TEQUILA
A Traditional Art of Mexico

Edited by Alberto Ruy-Sánchez
and Margarita de Orellana

Guest editor: Eliot Weinberger

Published in association with
Artes de México

Smithsonian Books
Washington

Published in 2004 in the United States of America
by Smithsonian Books
In association with
Artes de México
Córdoba 69
Col. Roma
06700, México, D.F.
Tel. 52 (55) 55 25 59 05
artesdemexico@artesdemexico.com

ISBN: 1–58834–213–1

Library of Congress Control Number: 2004107325

Printed in Hong Kong
not at government expense.

10 09 08 07 06 05 04   1 2 3 4 5

Product of the most refined alchemies...it is a drink for the initiated, a test for distinguishing appearance from reality. Tequila tastes like its name. Vicente Quirarte

Contents

Pages 8–9
Jaime Sadurní.
Oil on canvas.

Pages 14–15
Jaime Esparza.
Barcelona, 1945.
Oil on canvas.
Both collection
of José Cuervo.

Tequila:
A Rite of Passage

Alberto Ruy-Sánchez

When you have a drop of tequila on the tongue, it is like a concentrated universe. Not everyone can sense that universe enclosed within tequila's fiery flavor, but it is there waiting for anyone able to decipher it. And this book describes that universe in detail. 🌵A little over two hundred years ago, the word Tequila was just the name of a small town in the Mexican countryside. One of many similar small communities, Tequila is located between Guadalajara and the port of San Blas on the Pacific coast. The region is crisscrossed by ravines and has a climate that is ideal for agriculture. The local alcoholic beverage used to be known as *vino mezcal*, or mezcal wine, and was one of a number of distilled spirits made in Mexico using a Arabic invention imported by the Spaniards: the still. 🌵The plant providing the juice that is fermented and later distilled is a species native to the New World: the agave. And the region of Tequila produces a very special variety of this plant that goes by the horticultural name of *Agave tequilana Weber*, blue variety. This species gave rise to Mexico's typically Mestizo beverage that can now be found throughout the world. 🌵Fields of blue agaves with their long sharp leaves—spiky bouquets that seem to want to stretch up and pierce the sky—offer an unusual panorama: a beautiful but sinister landscape. The fact that it is forbidding as the deepest jungle but clearly dominated by humans makes it even stranger and more paradoxical to our eyes. 🌵The history of industry and business in Mexico is closely linked to this word, as is the name of a tequila producer, José Cuervo, which is the oldest recorded Mexican company still in operation. It is also one of the most dynamic and influential firms in the country. But tequila's corporate aspect is not enough to explain how that beverage and not one of the other ones produced in Mexico came to symbolize the entire nation. A country's cultural life always sprouts up in the most unusual places and ways. Over the centuries, tequila first began to impregnate the nation's cantinas and much later, its homes, as the beverage that rich and poor alike could make their own. It provided the unity and sense of belonging needed in a country divided by huge economic differences and by generalized ethnic and social pluralism. 🌵The Mexican movie industry had its first real boom in the 1930s thanks to a subgenre known as the *Comedia ranchera* (along the lines of the Hollywood Western), which inevitably placed a bottle of tequila in the hand of every mariachi, as the drink that intensified the happy or anguished tone of his songs. Around the country and the continent, moviegoers saw how tequila accompanied the stars through the torments of love and their attempts at seduction, often carried out in song and while mounted on horseback. Tequila became a part of Mexican music, painting and literature. With wonder and great humor, it continues to make its reappearance in stories, novels and poems. And with a healthy dose of melodrama, it has played a role in certain Mexican soap operas—the famous *telenovelas*. In time, tequila finally made its entrance into the quiet dining rooms of more than a few respectable homes, especially at Sunday family gatherings. It is the obligatory aperitif, along with its inseparable companions of salt, lime and *sangrita*. The latter is an enigmatic beverage—red like blood, generally made with grenadine, orange juice, Cointreau and chilies, and not with tomato juice as most people think. Drinking tequila is a ritual to loosen the tongue, whetting one's appetite even as it fuels the conversation. Tequila has even been added to main dishes and desserts, defining new directions for Mexican Nouvelle Cuisine. It gives certain foods such as shrimp an unexpected intimacy, creating a new cultural existence so perfectly suited to them that we are surprised not to have thought of it before. There have recently been a number of new brands added to the upper end of tequila's price range, for which reason bottle design has become more and more inventive. There are even collectors specializing in tequila bottles. So, from the name of a town to industrial design, by way of our national identity, corporate and industrial history, the media, music, literature, as well as culinary tradition and innovation, tequila is much more than a distinguished beverage: it is a cultural phenomenon with multiple ramifications. There is a ritual to drinking tequila, and some basic knowledge that will help the novice make an easy entrance into the world of tequila connoisseurs. First, it is important to learn about the three basic tequila types, then to distinguish the purity of different brands, and finally to identify which one is the best suited to the body of the person drinking it. Tequila is a true adventure in taste and distinction—an adventure that begins and ends on the tip of the tongue as it tastes and discovers tequila's flavorful secret, its interesting concentration of practices and history, of creation and tradition. Tequila is clearly one of the most delectable and evocative arts of Mexico. *Translated by Michelle Suderman.*

20 Questions about Tequila

Margarita de Orellana

The following questions sum up those points that have most piqued the curiosity of both Mexican and foreign tequila lovers. The answers to these questions will provide you with the sufficient knowledge to join the ranks of true tequila connoisseurs.

1 What is tequila?
2 What does the word tequila mean?
3 How did tequila originate?
4 What is blue agave?
5 What is a *jimador*?
6 How are agaves grown?
7 What are agave *piñas*?
8 How is tequila manufactured?
9 What kinds of tequila are there?
10 What does 100-percent agave mean?
11 Is tequila agave the same as the maguey used to make *pulque*?
12 Does tequila come with a worm in the bottle?
13 What is the difference between tequila and mezcal?
14 What is tequila's denomination of origin?
15 When and where were the first distilleries established?
16 When did the exportation of tequila begin?
17 What are the functions of the Tequila Regulatory Council?
18 What is a *caballito*?
19 What is a margarita?
20 Which is the best tequila?

What is tequila?

A Mexican drink.

A spirit with the distinctive flavor of the distilled juice of wild plants, it is like the water of a burning river.

Tequila is derived from a plant that has indelibly marked the Mexican countryside: the blue agave.

It is a distillation of tradition: to drink it is to absorb stories and to be initiated into a world of legends.

Tradición

What does the word

tequila mean?

It is the name of a valley in the state of Jalisco where the drink has been produced for centuries. It is also the name of a mountain and of the town where several distilleries are based.

The Náhuatl origin of the name (*tequitl*, job or trade; and *tlan*, place) signifies a place of work and also the specific task of harvesting plants.

The word *tequio* refers to the labor of peasants.

Tequila came into being as a Mestizo creation during the initial decades following the conquest of Mexico: its pre-Hispanic ancestor was the American agave, used to produce fermented beverages even before colonization.

Its Arabic and Spanish ancestry contributed the process of distillation in the alembics or stills which had recently been introduced to the American continent. For many years it was known as mezcal wine or tequila mezcal, since mezcal or *mexcal* was one of the names given to agave.

How did tequila originate?

What is blue agave?

Agave tequilana Weber, blue variety, is one of the 136 species of agave that grow in Mexico. Its distribution around the country is likely due to the migrations of ethnic groups that domesticated it over the centuries. The Swedish botanist Carl Linnaeus baptized the genus in 1753, taking its name from the Greek word meaning admirable or noble. Some poets describe it as having a wondrous form: a secret root stretching its leaves toward the sky like a multipartite exclamation. The blue variety is used to produce tequila and is distinguished by the blue tinge of its leaves which grow in a roseate arrangement, and by the numerous shoots put out by the rhizome (a horizontal underground stem). It was classified by a botanist named Weber early in this century, which is why it bears his name. When the agave matures, a very tall flower stalk known as the *quiote* grows from its center. Flowering brings the plant's life to an end. Tender quiotes are eaten as a vegetable. Blue agave grows mainly in the municipalities of Amatitán, Arenal, Tequila and Hostotipaquillo; in the northeastern part of the Ameca region; and in Los Altos of Jalisco, in towns such as Atotonilco, Zapotlanejo, Totolán, Arandas, Jesús María and Tepatitlán.

Weber

What is a jimador?

The fleshy leaves of the agave must be cut off to obtain the plant's heart or *piña* which, when cooked, provides the juices that form the basis for tequila. The work of cutting the leaves and underground stem is called *jima* and the man who carries it out is the *jimador*. He uses a long-handled tool similar to a hoe called a *coa*. According to Don Ceferino—now sixty, but one of the fastest jimadores in the region in his youth—to be good at this job you have to have the right touch for cutting the leaves off the heart. It must be done with a single stroke, at the same height on each leaf, because if you don't know how and you cut higher up you have to cut twice as many times to even it out. We call this *coyazo*, which means not cutting again in the same place," he says. Jimadores can assess agaves just by looking at them: they can tell whether they have shrunk and are ready for cutting, or if they are too mature, diseased, and so forth.

Cultivation requires clay-rich soil in a semi-arid climate with a temperature that remains stable around 68°F. Agave is grown at some 5000 feet above sea level under skies that are overcast 70 to 100 days of the year. At the beginning of the rainy season, agave sprouts or babies are removed from the parent and planted in tilled land. The fields are plowed once a year, and the fleshy leaves of the agave are pruned leaving only those encircling the heart; this task is called *barbeo* or barbering. Plants mature in seven to ten years, but growing cycles vary from region to region, and even on the same plantation. Cultivating techniques have remained unchanged for centuries. Traditional tools for cutting leaves, such as *coas, barretones, casangas* and machetes, are indispensable and it is still common for workers to hand down the skills of their trade from generation to generation.

How are agaves grown?

What are
agave piñas?

When the leaves have been cut off, what is left is the *piña* or heart, which the jimador separates from the root. Before the leaves are cut off, the heart's weight cannot be determined with any certainty. According to jimador Don Ceferino, some weigh over 300 pounds. Once the piñas have been trimmed, loaders carry them from the fields to the vehicles that will take them to the factory. Even carrying them requires knowledge and skill. In Don Ceferino's words, "If a loader doesn't know how to lift them, if he hasn't got the experience or the knack, he won't be able to do it. We always carry the piñas on our heads, and it's a long way to walk. It's easier on the factory yard because the ground is hard concrete. But in the fields during the rainy season your foot can sink into the mud or you can slip." Once at the factory, the hearts are piled in front of the ovens. Other workers cut them in halves or quarters and load them into the ovens to cook, which will convert their starches into sugars.

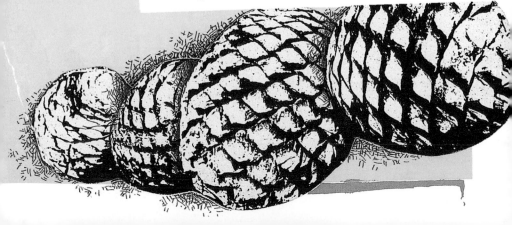

How is

tequila

manufactured?

Once the agave hearts have been cooked, either in ovens or autoclaves (which operate like pressure cookers), they are placed in crushing mills. The juice or must obtained is fermented in special tanks. If it is not 100 percent agave tequila, this juice is mixed with other types—particularly sugarcane—and they are fermented together. Fermentation converts the sugar into ethyl alcohol. The fermented juices then pass into stills, where they are heated to a high temperature to evaporate and then condense back into a liquid that can already be called tequila. However, it still contains impurities at this stage and so must be distilled a second time. The result is top quality blanco tequila.

Pure tequila is made entirely from agave. When the label does not specify "100% agave," the tequila is *mixto* (mixed). This means that a proportion of the sugar extracted from agave has been combined with other sugars during the manufacturing process. The tequila most commonly consumed, especially in the United States, is mixto. For many years Mexican standards permitted tequilas to contain a minimum of 51 percent agave and up to 49 percent other sugars. However, for some time now, industry norms have stipulated that the drink must be at least 60 percent agave to be called tequila. Some factories, Herradura for example, pride themselves on always having produced 100 percent agave tequila. As the prestige and popularity of tequila have grown, more and more factories have opted for maximum purity as a gauge of quality. The quality of *mixto* tequilas depends on the ingredients used. The Tequila Regulatory Council, an organization made up of agave growers, tequila producers and the government, supervises the quality of each tequila. Only a certificate issued by this council guarantees that a given product is truly 100 percent agave, bottled on-site and either reposado or añejo.

What does 100% agave mean?

There are three basic styles of tequila: *blanco, reposado* and *añejo*. Blanco or white tequila is as clear as water and is a finished product following the second distillation. Many connoisseurs prefer it because of its pure flavor. Reposado or "rested" tequila is the result of storing white tequila in oak or holm oak barrels for at least two months. It tends to have a somewhat woody color, and it is slightly smoother in taste than blanco tequila. Reposado is the most widely consumed of the three. Añejo or aged tequila is matured for at least a year in oak or holm oak barrels. It is darker than reposado tequila, and its woody flavor is more pronounced. For first-time drinkers, this is perhaps the most recommendable. Each factory makes variations of the three styles. Some add water, flavoring or coloring and call the resulting tequila *abocado* (sweet or mild).

What kinds of tequila are there?

blanco

reposado

añejo

Is tequila agave the same as the maguey used to make pulque?

No. Maguey, from which pulque is extracted and fermented, is a different type of agave—*A. atrovirens Kawr* or mild agave. It was widely used in pre-Hispanic times, and codices record seventeen different forms of this plant. The Mexica fertility goddess Mayahuel was said to have changed into a maguey, thus coming to symbolize the continuity of life. Pulque was a ritual drink in ancient times. It is produced by the fermentation of maguey juice (*aguamiel*) extracted directly from the plant and is still consumed today. Tequila is not made from aguamiel or pulque as many believe. It is distilled from the sugar-rich juices of the cooked hearts of another species of agave, *A. tequilana Weber*, which has narrower, more rigid leaves and a stronger blue tinge.

Does tequila

come with *a worm* in the bottle?

The maguey worm inside some bottles is characteristic of certain mezcals, never of tequila. Mezcal producers maintain that because the worm feeds on the agave plant, it contains a concentrated essence of the plant, and thus serves to enhance the flavor of the bottled liquor. There are red and white worms, the latter being the most highly valued. Worms are collected and bred on mezcal plantations, while in agave fields for tequila production they are regarded as pests to be destroyed because they weaken the plants.

Mezcal is made from several different varieties of agave with such names as *limeño*, *raicilla*, *pata de mula*, *bovicornuta* and *cupreata*, among others. Tequila is made only from *Agave tequilana Weber*, blue variety. Mezcal is considered to be ready for consumption after a single distillation, whereas tequila requires at least two, and is carefully filtered to eliminate impurities and to mellow its taste. Mezcal tends to have a more concentrated color and a more potent flavor from the outset. It often tastes smoky as a result of the custom of baking the piñas underground in a pit kiln. This flavor is in fact considered to be one of its desirable traits.

What is the difference between tequila and mezcal?

What is tequila's
denomination of origin?

With the growing consumption of tequila world-wide, several countries began selling other spirits as tequila. Mexican producers persuaded the government to stipulate that only the drink made with *Agave tequilana Weber*, blue variety, according to certain quality standards could be called tequila. By law, it is produced exclusively in certain areas of Mexico, including all of Jalisco and parts of Michoacán, Guanajuato, Nayarit and Tamaulipas. Efforts have been made for many years to achieve international recognition for these measures, as has occurred in the case of cognac, for example. In May 1997, Mexico signed an agreement with the European community to respect tequila's denomination of origin.

When and where were the
first distilleries
established?

There are no records of the first tequila stills. However, in 1538 the governor of New Galicia—an area that included what is now the state of Jalisco—issued a law to control the production of "mezcal wine." We know that in the eighteenth century, Pedro Sánchez de Tagle expanded agave cultivation in the valley of Tequila and legally established a distillery or *taberna* at the Hacienda de Cuisillos. In 1758 the Cuervo y Montaño family founded a distillery on the Arriba hacienda. In 1785, Viceroy Matías de Gálvez persuaded the king of Spain to prohibit the production and sale of intoxicating beverages, a measure that was enforced for ten years. When the law was abolished in 1795, José María Guadalupe de Cuervo set up a distillery at La Cofradía de las Ánimas, later to be called La Taberna de Cuervo. This was the origin of the company now known as Casa Cuervo or José Cuervo. The Tequila Sauza company dates back to 1873 and Tequila Herradura to 1870.

SUPREMO VINO TEQUILA

"San Andrés"

Hacda. de San Andrés.
Estación la Quemada
Jalisco

Marca Industrial Registrada núm. 24323.
GARANTIZADO ENTERAMENTE PURO
POR
ERNESTO A. ORENDAIN.
FABRICANTE.

When did
the exportation
of tequila begin?

Beginning in the sixteenth century, distilleries in the region of Jalisco (New Galicia) sent their product to the principal cities and mining areas of what is now Mexico. It was transported overland to fairs in other regions and also to seaports—in particular that of San Blas, Jalisco, founded in 1768. In 1792, a traveler named José Longinos Martínez wrote a diary of his journey from Mexico City to San Blas, in which he notes that the countryside between Amatitán and Tequila was covered in agaves and that thousands of barrels of mezcal wine were shipped out of there every year. Around 1870, tequila began to arrive in the United States by cart. The railroad speeded up the growth of the tequila market, and the industrial modernization of the major distilleries affected the level of exportation. Today, tequila is one of Mexico's main commodities sold abroad.

This nonprofit association established the guideline that to be called tequila, a given liquor must contain a minimum of 38 and a maximum of 55 percent of alcohol by volume (between 76 and 110 proof). The Council's principal activities include the registry and supervision of all brands of tequila manufactured in Mexico and even those bottled outside of the country. The latter can only be authorized by the Council if they are prepared using tequila from one of the registered producers in Mexico. Another of the Council's responsibilities is to take legal action against brands that violate these standards, which were published in the *Diario Oficial* of September 3, 1997.

What are the functions of the Tequila Regulatory Council?

What is a caballito?

This is a tall shot glass specifically for serving tequila. It has a characteristic cylindrical form, narrower at the base than at the top. Its origin is not certain, but its immediate predecessors are the bulls' horns used at tequila factories—also called *tabernas*—for tasting the spirit straight from the still. The caballito is a simplified glass version of those bulls' horns, which had their point cut off to be able to stand them on a bar or table.

What is a
margarita?

This is a cocktail prepared with tequila. It is served in a champagne glass with the rim dipped in lime juice and coated in salt. The drink consists of tequila blended with lime juice, Cointreau and crushed ice, but there are endless variations on this theme. This popular drink increased world consumption of tequila, particularly in the United States. There are many individuals and bars that credit themselves with the invention of the cocktail, both in Mexico and the United States. One of the most famous tales relates that a Texan woman named Margaret Sames served it for the first time to her visitors at her house in Acapulco. Another claims Carlos "Danny" Herrera from Tijuana created it in honor of Marjorie (Margarita) King, a beginning actress who could not drink any alcoholic beverage but tequila... and Cointreau. There are some bottled mixes on the market, but freshly made margaritas are always best.

Which is the
best tequila?

The final decision as to the best tequila always rests with the consumer. By selecting a tequila of guaranteed quality that you like, that meets all your expectations as to flavor and bouquet, harshness or smoothness, you can't go wrong. We recommend trying many different brands to discover the subtle differences among them, to form your personal preferences and even modify them as experience dictates. The key to a good tequila lies in the drinker's likes and dislikes. The opportunity of comparing different brands is what determines an individual's range of options. Enjoy the experience of enjoying tequila. Find your favorite tequila and share it, saying, "This is the best one," but never forget to add, "...at least, the one I like best."

el Mejor...

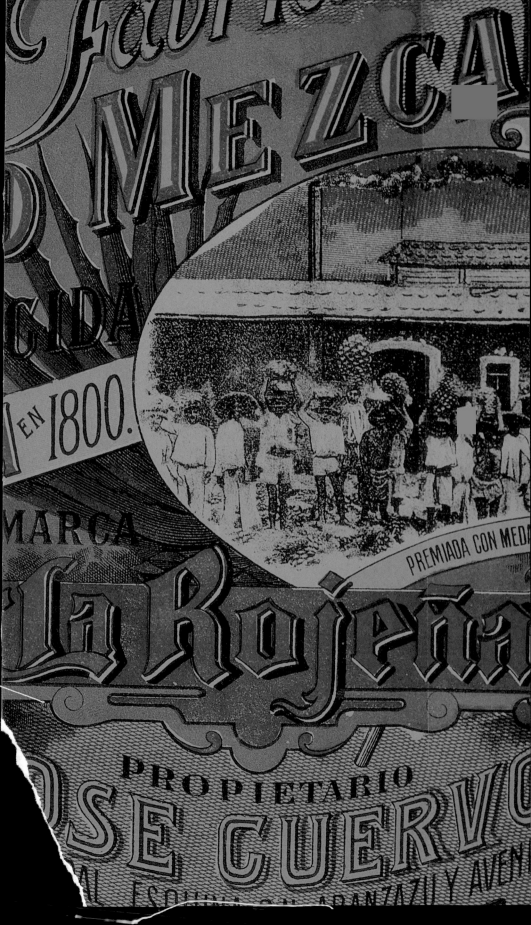

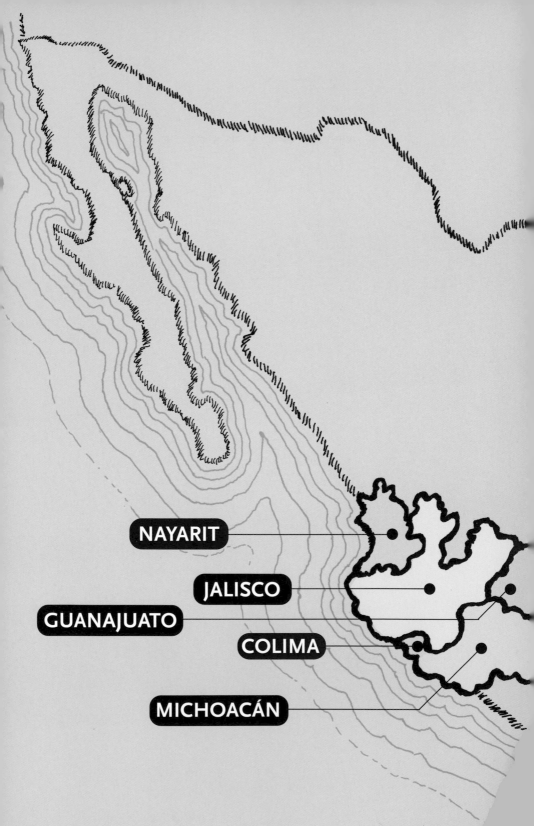

NAYARIT

JALISCO

GUANAJUATO

COLIMA

MICHOACÁN

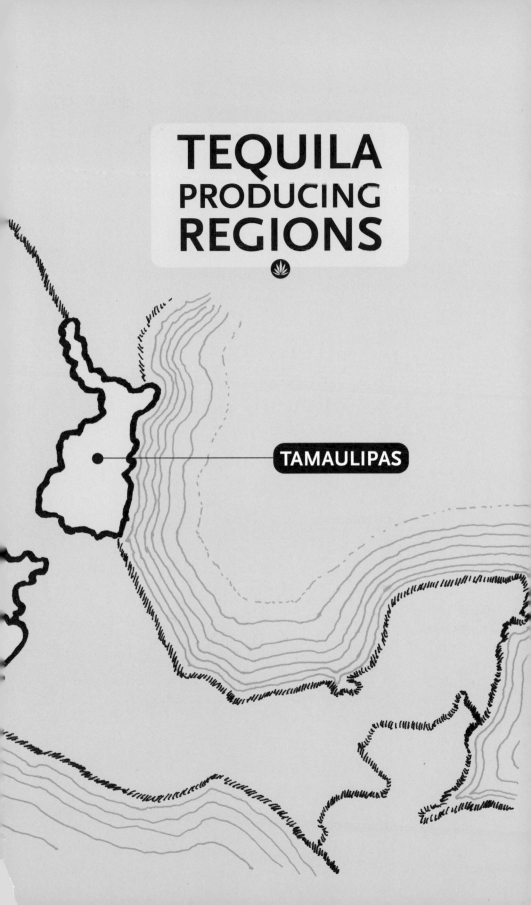

TEQUILA PRODUCING REGIONS

TAMAULIPAS

I

History of Tequila

Fermentation tanks for vino mezcal (as tequila was called before).

Tequila Moments

José María Muriá

Although the agave plant is not exclusive to Mexico, nowhere else is it more integrated into the landscape, and into the people's sensibility and lives. The agave (maguey) was called *metl* in Nahuatl, *tocamba* in Purépecha and *guada* in Otomí, but the word "maguey" came to us from the West Indies, on the lips of the conquistadors.

It no surprise, then, that in nineteenth-century Mexico—obsessed with the land and seeking the essence of what was "national"—the maguey constituted one of the most helpful elements for identifying a landscape as uniquely Mexican.

According to experts, there are more than seventeen varieties of agave. But more so than its botanical traits, this article will focus on the relationship between human history and the maguey, and how its alcoholic derivative, tequila, has shaped that history. Manufactured in the Jalisco region and considered the quintessential national beverage, tequila is consumed both domestically and internationally. Similar hard liquors produced from the maguey in other regions of Mexico are usually given the generic name of "mezcal" and are further distinguished by the name of the town where they were produced. Thus, we have mezcal from Oaxaca, Quitupan, Tonaya, Tuxcacuesco and Apulco. Nonetheless, tequila is considered the quintessential Mexican drink, just as the mariachis and *charros* (cowboys) of Jalisco exemplify Mexico's music and its people.

Tequila's Signs and Geography

From an etymological standpoint, there are various interpretations of the word "tequila." Most think the word comes from the Náhuatl *téquitl* (duty, job or task) and *tlan* (place), and refers to a site where certain tasks were performed. On the other hand, it could mean "the place of cutting," as Jorge Murguía notes in his *Toponimia náhuatl de Jalisco*, from the verb *tequi* which means "to cut, to work or to toil," according to Ángel María Garibay Kintana.

Nuttall Codex (sixteenth century). Some of the seventeen varieties of agave known in pre-Hispanic times.

Tequila, Jalisco, is a town of pre-Hispanic origin, a population center with more than 18,000 inhabitants, about sixty miles northwest of Guadalajara. Within the municipality, a peak that was once an active volcano rises nearly 10,000 feet above sea level, shaping the landscape. Tequila is also the name of the mountain valley where the town lies. But the word has not been confined to the geographical limits of the town. The town's importance in colonial times made it the capital of a district of the New Kingdom of Galicia, also bearing the name of Tequila. At the end of the eighteenth century, the magistracy—with almost the same borders—became a part of the mayoralty of Guadalajara.

At the dawn of Independence it was denominated a department; during the political upheavals of the nineteenth century, it was reduced to a smaller district, and then became a department again, until these geopolitical entities were abolished during the Revolution of 1910. It bears noting that the department coincided almost exactly with the tequila-producing region, before tequila-making began to spill over into neighboring areas. Finally, from 1872 to 1891, Tequila was also the name of the twelfth district of the state of Jalisco.

A Special Blend

In Náhuatl culture, the maguey was considered a divine creation, endowed with supernatural powers. According to Antonio Caso, the maguey was a representation of Mayahuel, the goddess who, like the Venus of Ephesus, had 400 breasts to feed her 400 children—the *centzon totchtin*. These innumerable gods and goddesses of intoxication were worshipped in various mountain communities and their names derived from the tribes of which they were the patrons.

"The maguey plant, or agave, was extremely important to the domestic economy, since its sap was fermented to make a kind of beer (*sic*), *pulque*," writes George C. Vaillant.

Bernardino de Sahagún.
Florentine Codex (sixteenth century).
Agave cultivation and harvesting.

This pulque was not only a liquor and ritual beverage, but also served an important nutritional function as it compensated for the lack of vegetables in the Mexican diet.

The Franciscan brother Toribio de Benavente, nicknamed Motolinía by the Indians, was deeply impressed by the variety of uses indigenous people found for the maguey, as noted in his *Memoriales* (Memoirs). Besides pulque, Fray Toribio admired "how they use those spears of *metl* to make thread for sewing, cords, rope, halters, saddle straps and rope headstalls,... clothing and shoes, which the Indians call *cactli*.... They also make soles for sandals like those from Andalusia, blankets and cloaks." Even the barbed spears were of great utility, according to the monk. He mentions that the dried leaves were used to roof homes, to make paper or simply to kindle fires whose ash "is very good for lye." Nor did he forget the curative properties of pulque and agave juice, as described in figure 596 of the Florentine Codex. Fray Juan de la Concepción, a

The Maguey Goddess (Mayahuel)
Ignacio Vértiz Gargollo

Mayahuel is the symbol of the earth's fertility. When she was transformed into a maguey plant, she bestowed on [Mexica] men the gifts required for survival. She is also the mother of the four hundred rabbits, or Centzon Totochtin, the four hundred or innumerable gods of drunkenness. The goddess had four hundred breasts to nourish her children. Mayahuel is a possible derivation of meyahual, the center of the maguey encircled by intertwined leaves, and refers to all her arms that flower for the same people. Mayahuel displays her naked torso; her quechquémitl blouse and her skirt are made of water and adorned with shells. Her headdress is also of water and with yellow feathers. At the center it has some figures of maguey from which emerges a braided rope, and opposite Mayahuel, a part of the maguey's flower stalk may be seen in bloom. She is the only divine personification to be characterized as nursing a non-human figure: a winged fish hanging from her breast.

The goddess Mayahuel. Codex Tonalámatl Aubin.

little-known discalced Carmelite, also described the wonders of the maguey. An octave from his "Romance histórico" is quoted by Lorenzo Boturini in *Idea de una nueva historia general de la América septentrional* (Outline for a New General History of Northern America): "Twisted fibers from the maguey/ Gave rise to many volumes of history/ In which the colors were pages/ Forming characters out of knots./ Brushes were better than quills/ To copy onto cotton the likeness/ Of divine heroes, who by touch / Judged objects by their massiveness."

It seems inevitable that a society so prone to associating anything good around it with divinity would deify a plant that provided them with so many things.

The fact that no source mentions any kind of intoxicating drink except for those that are simply fermented has led to the general conclusion that the process of distillation was completely unknown in pre-Hispanic Mexico. In this way, the use of the maguey's heart to make spirits is one of the most important products of the cultural blending that began when Spanish dominion was established in our Mexican lands.

News of Colonial Mezcal Wine

Motolinía did write something about the production of a liquor by cooking mezcal or the heart of the maguey, but like many texts of sixteenth-century New Spain, it is written in a manner confusing to today's readers. He wrote that he heard it called *mexcalli*, "which the Spaniards say is substantial and healthy." If this is true, then the so-called "mezcal wine" (*vino de mezcal*) was one of the first products obtained from native North American ingredients using European techniques. But it also seems likely that when the Spaniards came to what is now Jalisco, mezcal was still not produced in other parts of the Colony.

Nonetheless, there is no documentation from the first century of colonial life (descriptions, accusations, refutations and so forth) to suggest that mezcal wine was being produced in significant quantities. There is a reference, though unsubstantiated, that "in the year 1600, Pedro de Tagle, Marquis of Altamira and Knight of the Order of Calatrava, came to live in Tequila, and upon his arrival established the first mezcal wine factory in New Galicia." It does not concern us here whether Tagle actually came to Tequila, or if "he was able to amass a large fortune within a few years," as was also stated. Rather, it is important to note that he could not have been the first to manufacture mezcal in the magistracy of Tequila. He may, however, have been among the first producers of large quantities of mezcal wine for anything other than personal consumption.

In fact, the first reliable reference to tequila comes from *Descripción de la Nueva Galicia* by Domingo Lázaro de Arregui, written around 1621, in which he states that, "*mexcales* are similar to the maguey, and their roots and hearts are eaten roasted. From the roasted fleshy leaves, they are able to squeeze out a juice from which, little by little, they obtain wine, clearer than water, stronger than moonshine, and with the same flavor. And although the mezcal from which it is produced confers many virtues, the vulgar and excessive manner in which it is consumed debases the wine and even the plant."

Mexcales are similar to the maguey, and their roots and hearts are eaten roasted. From the roasted fleshy leaves, they are able to squeeze out a juice from which, little by little, they obtain wine, clearer than water, stronger than moonshine, and with the same flavor. **Domingo Lázaro**

An industry, however small, could only be established in a society with more sedentary habits and a larger population. Thus, it was not until the Spaniards were established in the New World and became Criollos that initial attempts could be made to manufacture mezcal wine on a larger scale than that required for personal consumption.

The village of Tequila is a good example of the shift in the source of wealth, from royal mines to agricultural work. In 1563, Tequila was no more than a small indigenous community, paying tribute to the Crown as part of the larger mayoralty of the mines of Xocotlán. Seven years later, however, Tequila was named capital of its own district and entered an economic upswing due to agriculture. This wealth—amassed through agrarian production, though more gradually than the riches brought by a lucky sword or pickax—was what converted the Spaniard into a Criollo and linked his life and fortune to the land. In this way, small and impoverished agricultural centers were transformed into productive haciendas. By the early eighteenth century, when

Guadalajara became the regional center, various economic activities became important. In his *Historia de la Nueva Galicia en la América septentrional* (History of New Galicia in Northern America, 1742), Matías Ángel de la Mota Padilla (1688–1766) mentions the prohibitions, reprimands and penalties imposed upon those who manufactured mezcal wine, distributed it or consumed it in excess. But he also indicates that the manufacture of this product increased in spite of all this.

With the failure of Prohibition, the authorities of Guadalajara decided to regulate the manufacture and sale of mezcal wine. In the 1640s, they ordered the creation of sufficient state stores to fill the coffers of the public treasury for funding public works projects. Over a rocky century, the state store system was solidified and lasted until its abolition by the independent government.

The Independent Traveler

The Guadalajara region largely emerged from isolation in the seventeenth century. Little by little, the northern Pacific coast began to develop and Guadalajara—the natural source of supplies due to its proximity—became aware of the new market and its benefits. On the other hand, the flow of goods from Asia also grew considerably in the mid-eighteenth century. Among other things, the Crown opened the auxiliary Pacific port of San Blas. Given that the tequila region lay midway between Guadalajara and San Blas, the port grew during the mid-1700s, and the area began to supply the new Spanish colonies in northeastern Mexico. "The mezcal wine of this land" soon became the primary export from what is now the state of Jalisco. The mezcal of Tequila aided the Spaniards in overcoming loneliness in the northern lands. In turn, it was also useful to Jesuits and Franciscans in their missionary duties, as it helped the Indians endure a lifestyle vastly different from that to which they were accustomed, while they waited with patience and resignation for Eternal Bliss.

Jimador (harvester) gathering agave piñas.

The town of Tequila also quenched the eager thirst of those who worked in the nearby Bolaños mines, which prospered toward the end of the eighteenth century. The "wine of this land" gained renown in Mexico City for its superior quality, even though other mezcals from nearby regions were sold in the capital at a much lower price. Many years would pass before the agaves of Tequila were recognized as a distinct species, though discerning palates could tell the difference even then. Still, there is little information about mezcal wine in the late eighteenth and early nineteenth centuries. Prohibition periodically disciplined the industry, so merchants and producers worked with local authorities who agreed to play down their profits.

When the struggle for Mexican Independence began, data on both the production and sale of tequila showed a considerable increase. From 1815 to the end of the independence movement, the industry suffered a marked decline, mostly because the port of Acapulco was reopened and San Blas again became an auxiliary port.

After 1821, mezcal producers, like most local businessmen, primarily wanted fewer trade restrictions in order to find an outlet for surplus production during the good years and for unsold product during leaner times. In the early nineteenth century, there were twenty-four ranches and haciendas—twelve in Tequila, twelve in Amatitlán—most of them rich in agaves. Thanks to a study by Ramón Charles Perles, we know that since 1795, "the wine of this earth" was produced on a large scale by José María Guadalupe on the Cofradía de las Ánimas hacienda, purchased in 1758 by his father José Antonio de Cuervo. This distillery, or *taberna* as it was also known, was inherited by the daughter of José María Guadalupe, María Magdalena Ignacia. In Tequila, she married Vicente Albino Rojas, who became the factory's administrator and later its heir.

During the entire nineteenth century, it was customary to name distilleries after their owners, adding the Spanish feminine suffix -eña to the family name. La Floreña, La Martineña, La Guarreña, La Gallardeña, La Quintaneña—all are names of factories which played an important role in the latter half of the nineteenth century.

On the other hand, other properties remained loyal to the liberal-positivist vocation, embodying the theme of order and progress, using names to communicate their convictions to the common man. The factory La Antigua Cruz (The Ancient Cross) was renamed La Perseverancia (Perseverance) by its new owner Cenobio Sauza, and Jesús Flores, owner of La Floreña, gave his business the name La Constancia (Constancy).

A decree dated October 3, 1835 forced greater provincial dependence on the capital. Through this ordinance, state legislatures were replaced by district boards, and governors had to report directly to the Mexican president. Those who had learned how to generate and handle their own resources, and return profits to their community during the ten federalist years, could not tolerate outside control of their economic activities and management by people in the distant national capital who would decide how investments had to be made.

The following decades proved ill-fated for the country, but without a doubt, the debacles of Texas independence, the U.S. invasion of Mexico and the French intervention helped forge nineteenth-century Mexico's identity and to accentuate its national spirit. French writer Ernest de Vigneaux noted in 1854, "Tequila lends its name to the mezcal liquor, in the same way Cognac does to the liquors of France." While many years would pass before the name tequila became common in the highest echelons of trade and industry, it is evident that the word already served to identify the mezcal wine manufactured in the region.

During the tumultuous events of the nineteenth century, there was no precise data available on mezcal pro-

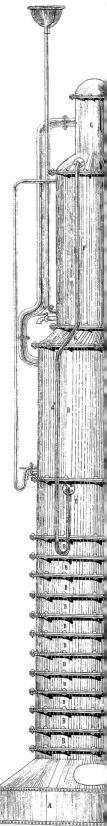

During the entire nineteenth century, it was customary to name distilleries after their owners, adding the Spanish feminine suffix "-eña" to the family name. La Floreña, La Martineña, La Guarreña, La Gallardeña, La Quintaneña—all are names of factories which played an important role in the latter half of the nineteenth century.

Unloading mezcal plants at La Constancia.

On the other hand, other properties remained loyal to the liberal-positivist vocation, embodying the theme of order and progress, using names to communicate their convictions to the common man. The factory La Antigua Cruz (The Ancient Cross) was renamed La Perseverancia (Perseverance) by its new owner Cenobio Sauza, and Jesús Flores, owner of La Floreña, gave his business the name La Constancia (Constancy). ❧

duction. Nor were there concrete figures on local financial assistance to the liberal armies, but one can examine troop movements and use other indications to see that the department of Tequila was prominent in the defense of the constitution and its reforms. With the restoration of the Republic and the consolidation of the liberal state, tequila-production matured into a true industry.

It is hardly surprising that a prominent tequila-producer, Antonio Gómez Cuervo, was named provisional governor and military commander of Jalisco, heading the first state government in the restored Republic. Gómez Cuervo did not miss an opportunity to protect his own interests or those of his staunch supporters, including fellow tequila-producers and his friend Ramón Corona. Without a doubt, this incipient industry owed its development to the man who, by hook or by crook (and with many setbacks), managed to be repeatedly installed in the government palace before finally retiring in 1871.

In January 1872, the government of Jalisco yielded to pressure from tequila-producers and ordered the establishment of a new district—number twelve—comprised of the old departments of Ahualulco and Tequila. The political leadership was headquartered in Tequila, a village which two years later would receive the title of city, "in reward for the patriotic and valiant conduct observed by its inhabitants" against the insurgent troops of Manuel Lozada, the legendary rebel leader who was known as "the Tiger of Álica."

Revolutionary Tequila

In spite of its history, Tequila and its neighboring region inexplicably declined around the turn of the century. Upper-class Mexicans' taste for all things French was tequila's foremost enemy. Francophilia reached such an extreme that tequila-drinkers could only be found among the *populacho*, or masses. Nonetheless, tequila consumption grew considerably.

In the end, it was the Mexican Revolution that promoted a new attitude which popularized tequila. With the defeat of General Porfirio Díaz's long-lived dictatorship in 1911, Francophilia was also relegated to the past, and the entire country embarked on a search for native expressions and customs to strengthen the Mexican identity. 🌿

Joel Rendón. Linocut from a series on tequila (detail). 1994.

In the end, it was the Mexican Revolution that promoted a new attitude which popularized tequila. With the defeat of General Porfirio Díaz's long-lived dictatorship in 1911, Francophilia was also relegated to the past, and the entire country embarked on a search for native expressions and customs to strengthen the Mexican identity. Drinking tequila as opposed to imported liquors became one of those gestures, but it went even further. The government itself consciously portrayed tequila as a symbol of the nation. The Mexican film industry, in its heyday in the 1930s and 1940s, also contributed greatly to this image, promoting particular stereotypes of what Mexicans were like and what they did.

Like many popular songs of the era, the movies played an important role in establishing tequila's increasing fame. Rumors that it was the best remedy to counter a Spanish Flu epidemic that was spreading through northern Mexico around 1930 had a lot to do with it, and were instrumental in creating a market for small bottles that were manufactured in the industrial city of Monterrey as an option to distributing tequila from unwieldy casks. At the same time, the petroleum boom on the Gulf coast of Mexico boosted tequila consumption, thanks to the introduction of pint flasks that were easy to handle and to carry.

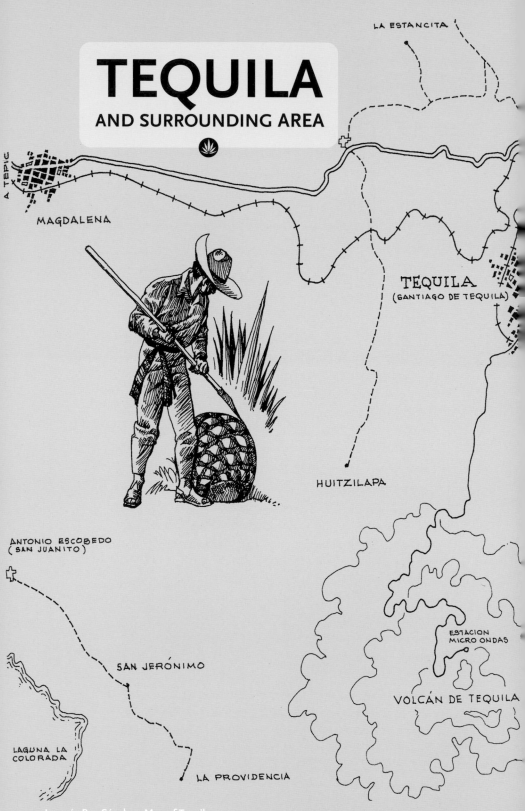

TEQUILA
AND SURROUNDING AREA

A TEPIC

MAGDALENA

LA ESTANCITA

TEQUILA
(SANTIAGO DE TEQUILA)

HUITZILAPA

ANTONIO ESCOBEDO
(SAN JUANITO)

ESTACION
MICRO ONDAS

SAN JERÓNIMO

VOLCÁN DE TEQUILA

LAGUNA LA
COLORADA

LA PROVIDENCIA

Joaquín Ruy Sánchez. Map of Tequila. 1994.

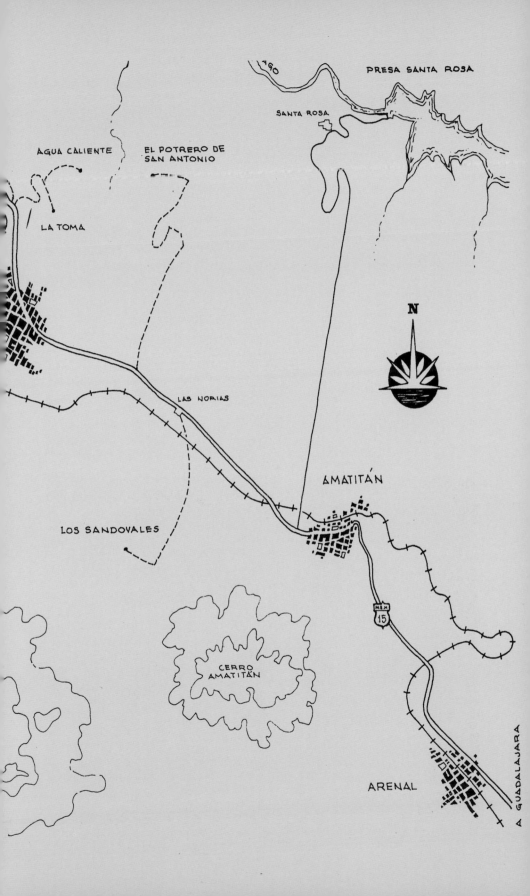

PRESA SANTA ROSA

SANTA ROSA

AGUA CALIENTE

EL POTRERO DE
SAN ANTONIO

LA TOMA

N

LAS NORIAS

AMATITÁN

LOS SANDOVALES

MEX
15

CERRO
AMATITÁN

ARENAL

A GUADALAJARA

Panoramic view of the town of Tequila. *ca.* 1940.

Parade ground in Tequila, Jalisco. *ca.* 1940.

In the 1940s, the tequila industry was ready to compensate for the lack of whiskey whose importation ceased in the United States during the Second World War. Tequila exports reached dizzying heights. However, the rapid decline that came with armistice forced the industry to make great efforts to expand the domestic market and look for consumers abroad.

In the 1950s, tequila began to be produced with the best technology then available. Many factories had to find ways to maintain high production levels without sacrificing quality, especially since certain brands with lower alcohol content were more appealing to the average consumer. Moreover, producers were able to meet increased demand once they learned that the region where blue agave was cultivated could be extended without affecting quality. However, it is unfortunate that despite many international accords and conventions—which state that tequila may only be manufactured in designated regions of Mexico—counterfeit tequila is produced in several countries whose governments look the other way.

Today, a vast central region of Jalisco is covered with the distinctive landscape of agave fields. Directly or indirectly, the industry employs some 300,000 people who are proud to participate in the manufacture of a product so tied to the life of western Mexico, and honored to offer a truly Mexican drink to the rest of the world. Tequila has a long and tumultuous history, closely linked to that of its region of production. It is clearly a cultural hybrid and a rural inhabitant like the people of Jalisco themselves. It has a semiclandestine and anarchic past. When it tried to escape urban condemnation, it underscored its uncompromising regionalism in the face of New Spain. Populist, federalist and liberal in the nineteenth century, and a drink for the masses according to Europeanized nineteenth-century tastes, it soon became a truly revolutionary and nationalistic drink. *Translated by Sara Silver.*

Peeled agave hearts (*piñas*).

How Tequila Was Made in the Old Days

José López Portillo y Rojas

This is the oven. To cook the mezcal, build a pyramid of firewood at the bottom and light it. Arrange the split agave hearts around it symmetrically, until they reach the top and are level with the ground. Cover the oven immediately. After cooking, remove the roasted mezcal, which has changed color in the process, its white color turning dark yellow.

Pages 72–79: Luis Vargas. Illustrations of the old tequila manufacturing process.

Once the mezcal is cooked, it is taken to the *tahona* or mill, a circular area covered in masonry with a large, extremely heavy stone wheel on an axis. The crude machine is moved by a team of oxen. The wheel, the oxen and the driver —barefoot and with his pants rolled up to his knees—go around and around the tahona, grinding and crushing the mezcal to extract the syrup it contains, which soon fills up the tahona.

The workers collect that syrup together with the *bagazo*, or fibrous pulp, in large buckets that they empty into huge barrels. In several days, once fermentation has taken place, the must is removed and poured into pots designed for making alcohol, which are set into wide stone and limestone benches. There are ovens with hot fires beneath each of them.

When the must boils, the alcohol evaporates and is deposited on the outside surface of the bottom of an iron or copper kettle placed a certain distance above the pot. This kettle must always be kept cold by means of a stream of water bathing the upper part. This condenses the alcoholic vapor and the steaming liquid can run down a conduit attached to the metallic rim. The resulting spirit is the famous *aguardiente de Tequila*, which, when drunk warm, is sweet to the taste and does not burn the mouth. It is very intoxicating and is known as *tuba*. *Translated by Michelle Suderman.*

José Cuervo's house. Guadalajara, Jalisco. It is now a post office.

A Micro-History of Tequila:
The Cuervo Case

Margarita de Orellana

José Antonio de Cuervo and his sons, José
María Guadalupe and José Prudencio, never
dreamed that the hundreds of blue agave
plants they cultivated in the eighteenth century would become millions as time went by. Nor could
they guess that they were to be remembered as the
founders of a tequila-producing dynasty, at the head of
the oldest company in the business and one of the most
successful. The Cuervo *taberna*, or distillery, has changed
names more than once over the last two hundred years.
But as it turned out, each of its proprietors made contri-
butions not only to the family business but to the history
of tequila itself, and to the history of the region.

It is known that the mezcal plant was initially harvest-
ed in three small valleys of New Galicia: Amatitlán, Arenal and Tequila. There is still no decisive evidence as to
exactly when the Spaniards first distilled the local agave
juices. Historian José María Muriá writes that in 1621, reference was made to an abundant agave harvest despite
the prohibition on making alcohol from this and other
sources. He also tells us that towards the middle of the
same century, agave cultivation was regulated, largely to
create a state monopoly and accrue more taxes. In the
long run this was highly profitable for the public works
then under way in Guadalajara. Such taxes continued to
be collected throughout the eighteenth century and part
of the nineteenth, and even during the strict prohibition
decreed by Charles III of Spain between 1785 and 1795.
These tributes must have reached considerable sums, as
we can deduce from Mota y Padilla's plan in the mid-
eighteenth century to partially fund the construction of
the University of Guadalajara with tequila profits.

It is possible that the Cuervo company, which recently celebrated its 200th anniversary, is in reality far older. It
may indeed be one of the oldest firms in Mexico, perhaps having originated prior to 1795. We cannot even
know for sure whether José Antonio de Cuervo—who in

Antt.º Cuervo como Maior d.º de la d.ª Cofradia
ditas Animas de este Pueblo, Encuio Hombre tom[ó] [po]sse=
sion en la forma acostumbrada, y p.r este auto asi lo pro
bey mande y firme con los d mi assd.ª como d.hº es de que
doi fee =

Ju.n Lopez Bonillo
y Palindo

Phelipe Bonilla

Juan de Maria
Benites

Yn continenti en d.hº Pueblo d.hº dia mes y año, yo d.hº Coue
g.º en Virtud del auto que antese de p.r mi proberdo, y en con
formidad de los Instrumentos que D.n Joseph el Cuervo como
maior d.ºmo de la citada Cofradia de Animas sita en este Pueblo
me presento de lo que aparese el Remate que se le iso el dia
seis de Enero del año proxime pasado de sincuenta y sis, a
d.hª Cofradia de los citados dos pedasos de Tierra nomb
.dos Toyusca, y Tototoasco, y su aprovasion en el dia nueu
del mes de Noviembre del año de sincuenta y siete el que
se hizo con consentimiento de las partes; Pasé a dar la d.hª
posesion, la que en Hombre de SM.d que Dios guarde ma[s]
y puse en posesion en Hombre de la d.hª Cofradia de la Bendi

1758 purchased some land in what is now Tequila—had been cultivating agave since the early years of the century. Nor do we know to what extent he was affected by the decade of prohibition. However, there is no doubt that his son, José María Guadalupe Cuervo, was the first to obtain a "mezcal wine" production license from Charles IV in 1795, as soon as prohibition was lifted. Before this, in 1781, his brother José Prudencio had acquired lands from the Hacienda de Abajo, and this was where the Cuervo distillery was later situated. The lives of the Cuervo family and the history of the village of Tequila became entwined when José Prudencio got involved in the construction of the parish church, from 1771 to 1775. This fact leads us to suspect that although the Cuervos only received their manufacturing license in 1795, they had been making tequila at least since mid-century. The license represented an opportunity to expand the business, now that the product could be openly made and sold. One document from 1801 records the following: "As a subtenant of the cribas (receptacles) of the spirits of this soil during the last five-year period (1795–1800) and the present one (1800–1805), please Sir, state the number of cribas coming from this town...to which José Guadalupe replied, the number approximates 400,000 a year, each requiring the burning of three loads of firewood."

In 1805, José Guadalupe declared himself to be the owner of the distillery, the family house and twelve fields containing hundreds of thousands of mezcal plants, especially the species known as chinos azules (blue Chinese) and manolarga (longhand). The town of Tequila had grown into one of the wealthiest boroughs of the Guadalajara jurisdiction, boasting a church which was "surely the finest monument in the entire province," according to a late-eighteenth-century account.

When José Guadalupe died, he bequeathed all his property to his children, José Ignacio Faustino and María Magadalena de Cuervo. The latter married Vicente Albino

Rojas, offering him all her goods and chattels. According to Muriá, Rojas was an individualist—like so many tequila men—who could not tolerate having the business under his father-in law's name (Taberna de Cuervo), and rechristened it after himself: La Rojeña. Vicente managed his distillery with flair, and his fortune increased by leaps and bounds. He boosted production and distributed the mezcal wine not only within Jalisco state, but also to fairs and festivals as far away as Aguascalientes, Zacatecas and San Luis Potosí. In the mid-nineteenth century, La Rojeña was the most renowned of all the distilleries in Tequila and was cultivating three million agave plants. Vicente's grandson, José López Portillo y Rojas, wrote a nostalgic memoir called "Nieves" describing the payday ritual at the growing factory: "My grandfather, seated at the head of a colossal oak table with a scribe to his right marking off the lists, counted out each wage packet according to the sum announced by another employee. In a strong accent, this man would bark out the worker's name, the balance of his account and the amount owed to him in cash and kind (meat and corn). The table was always piled with sacks of coins of every denomination, while more coins tantalizingly filled a variety of open gourds and metal pans, causing the rustic laborers to cast furtive, respectful glances at this dazzling display of lucre. Other helpers distributed the corn, which was scooped out with a wooden bowl and leveled with a strickle. A quartered ox hung from the iron hooks of a portable frame. Its flesh, deftly sliced by a burly butcher, provided the coveted meat ration assigned to each employee by the loud cries of the announcer."

Like other distilleries of the region, La Rojeña was obliged to ride out the storm of political instability that lasted most the nineteenth century, which was plagued by constant wars and foreign interventions. López Portillo y Rojas records that his grandfather's fortune shrunk considerably through the extortion of one or another faction

"Lo de Guevara," a mezcal farm in the Tequila region. Property of José Cuervo.

Filling an oven at "La Constancia" factory with mezcal plants.

fighting the War of Reform. However, an account from 1843 describes the town of Tequila as follows: "Towers of smoke loom up on every side, disgorging great quantities of vapor into the air like gigantic monsters, while all around, the fields are sown with American agave."

In the nineteenth century, three men were responsible for the growth of the Cuervo firm: Vicente Albino Rojas, Jesús Flores and José Cuervo Labastida. Although the latter only took over in 1900, he had worked at the distillery during the latter part of the 1800s. All three entrepreneurs showed genuine concern for the small neighborhoods where their economic activity was centered. Distillation was the source of their wealth and the reason for the political power wielded by these localities. Other industrialists had developed similar power bases in the political life of Tequila and its environs.

Vicente was never to see the arrival of the railroad, with its many benefits. He died leaving everything to his daughters, Inés and María Rojas de López Portillo. They transferred La Rojeña to Jesús Flores, owner of two distilleries, La Floreña and La del Puente, later rebaptized La Constancia. We do not know precisely how or why La Rojeña passed into the hands of this new owner, but there is no doubt that he breathed new life into the industry, making it one of the most important in the region. Anticipating the effects of the coming railroad, Jesús Flores prepared. Having expanded the acreage under cultivation, he moved the ovens, mills, fermentation tanks and stills out of the old José Prudencio Cuervo building and to La del Puente. The installations were enlarged, merged and renamed La Constancia. When the railroad was built, it replaced the mule teams that had formerly transported La Constancia's tequila to regional fairs, and considerably increased the volume of liquor sent to the port of San Blas. From there it was shipped to other parts of the Mexican northwest and possibly to the United States. Flores was the first tequila manufacturer

Grafiche "CHIATTONE,, Milano

ESPOS

GRAN PREMIO

...era la firma del Signor
...ndico Cubuchi à me noto
li 10 Luglio 1933

Notaio Raoul Guidi

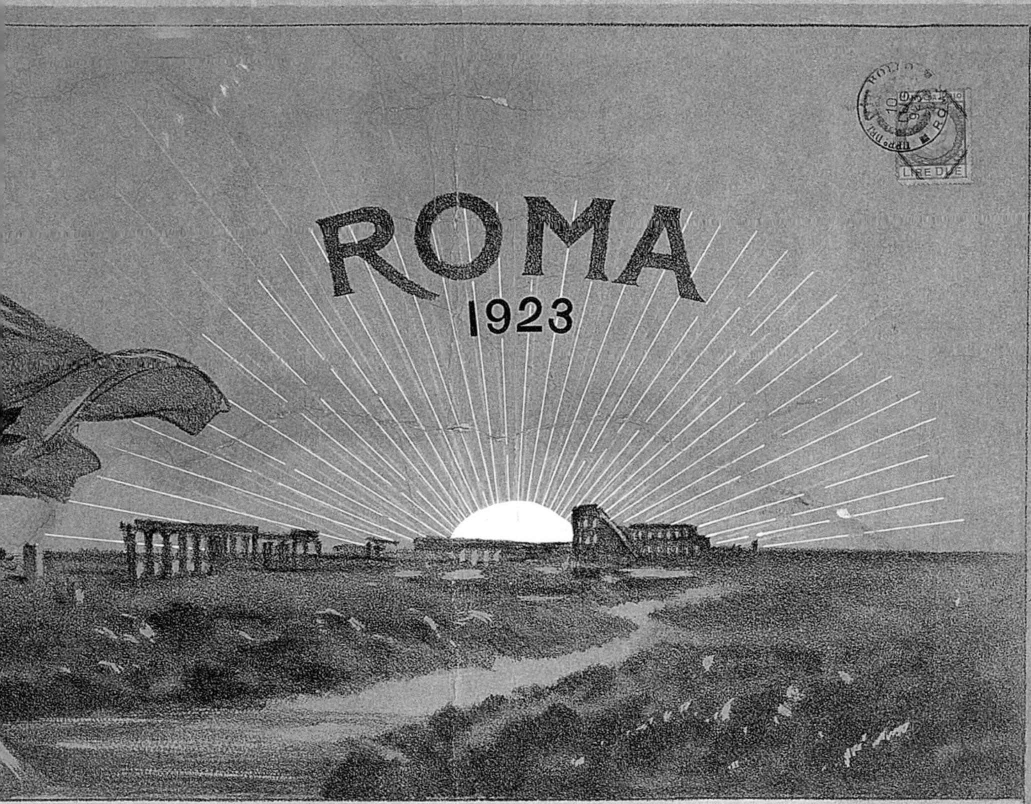

ROMA

1923

...ZIONE DEL PROGRESSO INDUSTRIALE

Mostre Campionarie – Réclame

DIPLOMA

DI GRANDE COPPA D'ONORE MEDAGLIA D'ORO

ANDE

José Cuervo Sucra . *Guadalajara Jal.*

por *Vino Tequila "Cuervo" marca "La Rojena"*

...TATO DIRETTIVO   DIRETTORE   PRESIDENTE DELLA GIURIA

Dott. Ugo F. Daneo

ESPOSIZIONE DEL PROGRESSO INDUSTRIALE
MOSTRE CAMPIONARIE RÉCLAME
ROMA
1923

MINISTERO DEGLI AFFARI ESTERI
SI ATTESTA L'AUTENTICITÀ DELLA FIRMA
DEL SIG. *Mortale*
ROMA 14 LUGLIO 1923
D'ORDINE DEL MINISTRO

Visto en este Consulado de Mexico
Se legaliza la firma del S. *Morane*
Roma Agosto 11 de 1923   p. el Consul. El Vice Consul
Nicolas Angelu

to introduce technological innovations into the distillation process. It was not long before the fruits of such investment and modernization began to become apparent. By 1880, he had sold almost 10,000 barrels (around 175,000 gallons) in Guadalajara alone.

Jesús Flores was the first to pioneer bottled tequila; previously, it had always been kept in wooden casks. In order to speed up the growth of the business, he hired staff to supervise the different departments, from cultivation to commerce and distribution.

In 1888, Flores remarried, this time to Ana González Rubio, whose sister Virginia was the wife of another tequila magnate, Luciano Gallardo, whose father owned La Gallardeña. For the next ten years, the couple saw their business prosper. In 1891, President Porfirio Díaz awarded them a certificate and a gold medal for the excellence of their tequila. Although they led a busy life in Guadalajara, they spent long periods in Tequila, enlarging their country property, today known as the Quinta del Refugio. Jesús Flores died at the age of seventy-two, leav-

José Cuervo's family. *ca.* 1900.

ing behind his wife who was the executor of his will and his sole heir. In 1900, Ana González Rubio found a new husband, José Cuervo Labastida, who had been the foreman at La Constancia. It was then that the tequila began to be called "José Cuervo" and the factory was restored to its old name of La Rojeña. José Cuervo, a descendant of the old patriarch, began to accumulate patents, awards and trademarks, including "José Cuervo's Great Mezcal Factory in Tequila," "Cuervo" and "La Rojeña." At the turn of the twentieth century, La Rojeña boasted four million mezcal plants grown on its various properties of Santa Teresa, Lo de Guevara, Camichines, Santa Ana, Las Cuevas, La Camotera, Los Colgados, La Fundición, El Colorado, Las Marías, San Pedro and Guamúchil. It owned 280 horses and mules for pulling wagons, and 112 teams of oxen.

The factory prospered under José Cuervo, winning some of the most prestigious international awards at the time, including the Gran Premio of 1907 in Madrid, and the Grand Prix at the 1909 International Food and Hygiene Exhibition in Paris, and ten others.

Marriage to José Cuervo had done little to change Ana González Rubio's day-to-day life. The couple had a new house in Guadalajara and still spent time in Tequila where they were popular figures, having been instrumental in bringing about the town's prosperity. In her memoirs, Ana's niece and future heir, Guadalupe Gallardo, recalls how the couple used to arrive in Tequila after a twelve-hour coach journey, during which the tired horses were periodically reinvigorated with the family product. The servants would fill their mouths with tequila and blow it up the animal's nostrils, to immediate effect.

"Upon their arrival in Tequila," writes Gallardo, "the whole town hall would be on hand to welcome my uncle and aunt. The next day, the priest would visit them with the latest parish news, and any pressing matters, closely followed by the commission and board of the hospital which they also patronized. José and Anita introduced piped water to the town and renovated the municipal and parish schools. They built covered wash-houses, redid the church floor, donated a public clock, laid an urban railway, paved the streets and enlarged the main square.... When the cemetery became overcrowded, José Cuervo purchased some property, walled it and gave it to the municipality on the condition that the poor might bury their dead there at no cost. The municipality overlooked the latter stipulation."

In light of all this, it is not surprising that José Cuervo had such a strong political influence in the area, as did his colleagues in the industry such as the Sauzas, the Romeros and the Orendains. Nor is it surprising that there were deep political differences between these families, causing frequent disputes and rivalries. One famous instance of this is the struggle between Liberal and Conservative factions led by the Cuervos and the Sauzas, respectively. All these prominent families opted to diversify their economies during the early twentieth century, once tequila had reached a high degree of mechaniza-

In the nineteenth century, three men were responsible for the growth of the Cuervo firm: Vicente Albino Rojas, Jesús Flores and José Cuervo Labastida. Although the latter only took over in 1900, he had worked at the distillery during the latter part of the 1800s. All three entrepreneurs showed genuine concern for the small neighborhoods where their economic activity was centered. Distillation was the source of their wealth and the reason for the political power wielded by these localities.

Stone oven with
blue agave *piñas*.
Collection of Donato Ruiz.

tion. Some invested in real estate, other in mining, tex-
tiles or flour mills. José Cuervo's Hacienda Atequiza
grew wheat, beans, corn and chickpeas as well as agave,
and also raised cattle.

During the first decade of the twentieth century, life in
Tequila went on as usual, hardly suspecting that economic crisis and revolution were just around the corner.
However, Guadalupe Gallardo hints that local tempers
were not as placid as they might seem: "No self-respecting gentleman was considered fully dressed without a
pistol in a nail-studded holster and a wide belt to carry
munitions. Scores were settled late at night, after observing the peaceful hour of the *serenata*. Though I recall
hearing frequent shots from the direction of the plaza, I
was always soothed by the catchphrase, 'It's nothing but
someone high on Dutch courage, firing into the air.'"

At this time, any tequila manufacturer who had not
modernized his methods and equipment was in deep
trouble. Jalisco's eighty-seven mezcal and tequila distilleries were reduced to thirty-two by 1910. La Rojeña had
no such problems, and was so important that its propri-
etor nearly became governor of Jalisco when Manuel
Cuesta Gallardo was forced to resign and was subse-
quently replaced by David Gutiérrez Allende. We can only
speculate about La Rojeña's potential wealth had Cuervo
been elected.

In 1914, the revolutionary forces were closing on
Guadalajara. Virginia Gallardo, future heiress to the
Cuervo fortune, married Juan Beckmann, the German
consul there. Beckmann formed part of the parliamen-
tary commission that negotiated the revolutionary
troops' peaceful entrance into the city by promising
wholesale surrender. The governor, federal army general
José María Mier, fled the city while his daughters took
refuge at the home of Virginia Gallardo. He later died at
El Castillo, during the rout of General Huerta's troops by
the revolutionary army.

According to Cuervo's first historian, Ramón Charles Perles, when the revolutionary troops occupied Guadalajara, not only did they consume huge quantities of Cuervo tequila, but confiscated whole cartloads of the stuff, as well. The fashionable drink at the time was the *torito de Jalisco* (tequila with fruit juice). General Julián Medina's men downed many of these before blowing up a certain railway bridge.

The year 1921 saw the end of José Cuervo's involvement in the tequila industry. After his death, Anita González Rubio was once more the sole head of the family business.

Four new entrepreneurs came on the scene during the twentieth century, living up to their predecessors' example in their intensified efforts to promote the industry's expansion. These men were Guillermo Freytag Schreir, his son Guillermo Freytag Gallardo, and the subsequent administrators and heirs of Cuervo, Juan Beckmann Gallardo and his son, Juan Beckmann Vidal.

When Lázaro Cárdenas began land redistribution in serious, many of Ana González Rubio's properties were affected. Her nearly 10,000-hectare hacienda at San Antonio del Potrero was reduced considerably. As a result of these changes, only eight distilleries remained in Tequila by 1929, including González Rubio's, two belonging to the Sauza brothers and five others. The 1930s did not bode well for the industry.

In 1934, Guadalupe Gallardo inherited the possessions of her Aunt Ana. Guillermo Freytag Schereir managed Tequila Cuervo until 1957. As foreseen, the decade of the 1930s turned out to be a tough one for many tequila companies. However,

The Cuervo family of the eighteenth century could never have imagined that what they had sown would provide for following generations. Today, the company continues in a race against time.

Cuervo survived until the market was reactivated with the advent of World War II. Guillermo Freytag Gallardo occupied the post of general manager from 1957 to 1964. He was followed by Juan Beckmann Gallardo—the grandson of tequila industrialist Luciano de Jesús Gallardo, as well as Guadalupe Gallardo's grandnephew—who directed the firm in the same entrepreneurial spirit as his predecessors. At her death, his mother Virginia Gallardo de Beckmann left everything to her four sons: Juan, Jorge, Carlos and Oskar. Today, Juan Beckmann Vidal has managed to maintain Cuervo's advantage over other tequila producers, especially with regard to exports, and is the driving force behind the technological advances that Cuervo has implemented in Jalisco. With a laboratory specializing in the micropropagation of agave, the company hopes to strengthen the plant and concentrate its sugar levels.

The Cuervo family of the eighteenth century could never have imagined that what they had sown would provide for following generations. Today, the company continues in a race against time. Tequila's popularity increases daily and the agaves continue to multiply. But Cuervo has another task ahead of it, and that is to write its own history, salvaging over two centuries of memories from the forgotten past. *Translated by Lorna Scott Fox.*

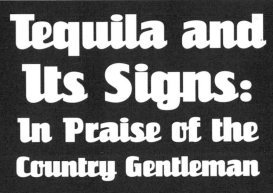

Tequila and Its Signs: In Praise of the Country Gentleman

Alfonso Alfaro

Tequila, like the nation, was born a bastard: a combination of American agave and European stills bearing the Arabic name of alambic. (Wine was always the drink of Spaniards or locally-born Criollos, while pulque represented the native world.) ✿

hat does a name taste like? How can lips and tongue decode, in a single gulp, dense symbols and forgotten stories that speak of so much care, so much rain, so many destinies blended into a single pleasure? Tequila is deceptively innocent. Its impalpable ingredient, pure to the point of invisibility, conceals a density of signs, charged with the opacity of time and memory.

Mexico is a fascinating metonymy: an immense and multifaceted country that has usurped the name of a single city and its locally circumscribed ethnicity. The Mexica founded a capital and an empire, on whose ruins the Spaniards erected a nation with far vaster contours, and so complex a nature that no Tenochca warrior could have identified with it. The ceaseless friction of centuries and signs has enabled this nation to define its identifying marks, emblems, stereotypes and distinctive frames of reference; and to construct a physiognomy that claims to predate all memories. Among its representative insignia, there is one that everyone can agree on: a refined elixir that on occasion nears the highest degree of perfection possible for manmade things. Why should a centralist state enamored of the Aztecs have chosen for its national beverage this liquor from a peripheral, coastal province, far removed from the Mexica world?

Tequila, like the nation, was born a bastard: a combination of American agave and European stills bearing the Arabic name of alambic. (Wine was always the drink of Spaniards or locally-born Criollos, while pulque represented the native world.) For the most part, the blue fields of agave were neither extensive estates nor small parcels. Somewhere between the vast inherited properties of wealthy families and the modest holdings of indigenous communities, they remained average-size haciendas or even large ranches, as in the case of properties elsewhere in Jalisco where other crops were cultivated. Following the colonial period, their owners tended to stick close to

Pages 108–109
Francisco Gálvez.
Roundup.
Oil on canvas. Jalisco.
Collection of M. Claudio Jiménez.

110

home, avoiding life in palatial surroundings, as they were less affluent and less powerful than the titled patricians of New Spain's viceregal court.

Of course, they never ceased to belong to a world of nobility, as we can see from their businesslike management of property, their patrimonial strategies, their severe code of behavior masquerading as simplicity and candor, and, above all, their unquestioned self-image.

Like the people who had amassed or inherited great fortunes, these comfortable landowners of European or mixed descent gradually built a homogeneous space where the tyranny of birth and blood lost some of its force, enabling it to become a matrix of the burgeoning Mestizo identity.

These country *hidalgos* (whether cattle ranchers, corn-growers or tequila producers) were invariably horsemen. It was in the rodeo-like rituals of *charrería* where they found their natural and distinctive expression. And in the transparent warmth of tequila, their palates recognized an aesthetic universe that was theirs alone, defined by the smell of earth, the sharpness of shadows etched by relentless light, terse phrases that needed no repetition, a world of emphatically male values and pleasures. There was much that these gentlemen held in common with their tequila: the open country, tradition, hard work, integrity and spiritual force.

The image of these country squires and that of the beverage that came to represent them were jointly admitted into the company of founding patriotic symbols. They were to contribute to the creation of stereotypes with which people of widely varying geographical and social origins could identify. Their Mestizo culture, attachment to the soil and solid family instincts made these gentleman farmers seem like familiar and charismatic figures to the peasantry and the nascent urban masses, lending them credibility as role models. At the same time, they found acceptance and kinship in the cul-

Francisco Alfaro.
Bullriding.
Oil on canvas. 24 x 29 1/2 in.
A. Cristobal Galleries.

tural world of the elite, thanks to their Spanish background, entrepreneurial values, gallantry and sense of honor. Thus an intermediary typology was born: less remote and controversial than that of the great landowners and Criollos in the wake of Independence and Revolution, less harsh and painful than the image of the Indian or *campesino.*

The nation had been founded with the help of a brutal process carried out by the citizens of New Spain and of Independent Mexico. They had ripped two images apart, one which celebrated imperial Aztec glory, the other representing the contemporary Indian. In this way they equipped themselves with something that demanded both loyalty and veneration. In this vast "fresco" that re-created and exalted a great but vanished civilization, all the inhabitants of the new motherland could find a part of themselves to be recognized and admired—traits that justified their pride in belonging. But while the sublimation of pre-Hispanic grandeur effectively gave rise to a political imaginary, the cultural imagination was demanding more familiar emblems that might be more suitable for a country that was changing so rapidly.

Societies like Mexico's, which are not entirely conditioned by traditional, communitarian systems of organization, nor by the cult of modernity based on the citizen as individual, include among their figureheads the image of the emancipated *paterfamilias*—lord of himself, his progeny and his properties. In this regard, the independent, enterprising, affluent country gentleman provides a starting point for the formation of a consistent stereotype: European with some Indian blood (or vice-versa), and a man who is the undisputed ruler of his fields and pastures, strict with his children and paternal toward his servants, pragmatic, self-assured to the point of stubbornness, valiant to the point of temerity, and relishing sensual pleasures of every kind; a pious Christian, yet unable to reproach himself for succumbing to the sins of the flesh.

The idealized vision of this tough, industrious man, king of his own castle, crept into the fantasies of the Mexican people during the early nineteenth century, when the country was still radically polarized between those sprawling estates and the indigenous communities. One Liberal ambition was to encourage the formation of a landowning economy, as the necessary prerequisite for a democratic society. The United States acted as both an incentive and an unattainable ideal in this respect. No doubt many people would have preferred the less labor-intensive farm system to that of haciendas and ranches, but agrarian legislation during the Reform period was clearly intended to promote the emergence of a class of small and midsized rural entrepreneurs. This utopia of a nation of landowners rapidly collapsed under the Liberal economic programs of the Porfirio Díaz regime—programs in fact designed to aid in its construction. The conversion of nontransferable lands into commodities only accelerated the growth of *latifundismo*, or large estates, and led ultimately to the Revolution. All hopes were destroyed by the very people who had promised to realize them, and optimism was overwhelmed by the violence of war. A new technological and cultural revolution would revive those hopes in the popular imagination, with a spontaneity that cannot be created either by force of will or by manipulation, in the same way as the alchemy of dreams.

During the golden years of cinema in the 1940s, Mexicans of every social class discovered their own "Rancho Grande"—an idyllic setting with flower-draped ranch houses, bursting granaries, fine horses and songs to stir the heart. This world was a far cry from both the moribund aristocracy of the large hacienda and the tiny plots of farmland that provided only struggles and deprivation. It was the vehicle whereby a country traveling the road to modernity and industrialization could manufacture memories to feed its nostalgia, a rural setting that could have been bucolic. This paradise succeeded in staving off ethnic and social antagonism and even mitigated certain conflicts at the root of this society's need to impose its images of paternal authority and manliness (as Octavio Paz has shown). The idealized prototype of the country gentleman with his mariachi music and his tequila—with which so many Mexicans sympathized or identified—became a common cultural reference thanks to the vast diffusion of movies that transcended social and territorial divisions, except in cases of extreme cultural marginalization.

Tequila thus became synonymous with these mythical lords of the screen: free, fierce, sensitive, frank, spirited and seductive. It conquered a place in the symbolic representations of the most diverse social sectors. Its taste and smell and its memorable body have transmitted these signals—and told all these stories—ever since. Even for those who have not yet enjoyed the experience, its three syllables evoke clarity and wholeness of character, the refinement of virile tenderness, the disturbing juices that await within the long razor-sharp leaves (an inspiration to Roland Barthes before he even tried it).

But, like fire, this firewater—the gift of mythological deities—houses a genie with a potentially savage smile.

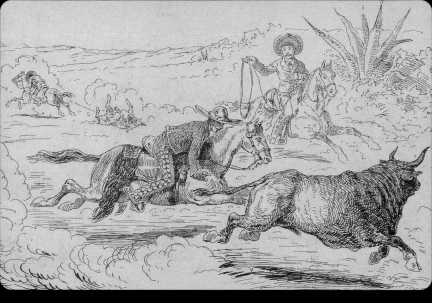

The idealized prototype of the country gentleman with his mariachi music and his tequila —with which so many Mexicans sympathized or identified—became a common cultural reference thanks to the vast diffusion of movies that transcended social and territorial divisions, except in cases of extreme cultural marginalization. Tequila thus became synonymous with these mythical lords of the screen: free, fierce, sensitive, frank, spirited and seductive. ⚜

Pages 116–117
Manuel Serrano.
Bull Tailing. ca. 1860.
Oil on canvas.
11 1/2 x 16 in.
A. Cristóbal Galleries.

In the magical obscurity of neighborhood bars or town squares, there materialized some of the most ancient and terrible phantoms of Mexican popular culture—those that associate alcohol with intoxication and pleasure with false euphoria.

Semiology alone—or how the elements of a cultural imaginary are represented—is not sufficient to explain the status enjoyed by tequila among the symbols of Mexican identity. At the same time that cinema reached its apogee, a genuine domestic market was being created in Mexico. The tequila industry was virtually unique in that it dealt with a distinctive, vernacular product, able to hold its own against the challenges of such a broad commercial space. Over the following decades, the tequila giants were equally alert and combative, ready for any adventure and profiting enormously from the market's gradual opening to the rest of the world.

Tequila thus underwent a new blending process in the alliance of two apparent contradictions: on the one hand, uncompromising standards of quality and traditional methods; on the other a modern attitude toward management, open to technological innovation, capable of devising bold strategies in the quest for new markets. It must now confront the obstacles that premature ambition and lack of historical perspective place in the path of any product based on prestige and excellence, and whose greatest long-term assets will always be the genuine quality of its raw materials and the authenticity of its manufacturing process. Owing to its rich heritage—combining its Mexican, Spanish and Arabic origins, as well as its symbolic references and entrepreneurial culture—tequila is now traveling to distant shores. It holds the keys to the gates of desire, although in every port and every neighborhood its symbolism may be interpreted differently. Abroad, the relationship between the two representations is seen even more plainly: the attributes of Mexico and those of tequila overlap, merging into a single image.

Francisco Gálvez.
Bullfighting. (Detail). 1872.
Oil on canvas. Jalisco.
28 3/4 x 37 in.
Collection of M. Claudio Jiménez Vizcarra.

It was in large part the movie industry that shaped stereotypes about Mexico in the popular imagination of the West, and thus led to their diffusion through a new mass culture on a global scale. Thanks to Margarita de Orellana's essay on the subject, we know of the crucial role played in the formation of these fantasies by American films on the Mexican Revolution. The Western made its own contribution, and today, whether in Burkina Faso, Bangkok or Bordeaux, every ordinary person harbors the same images of Mexico as a harsh, wild land, scorched by the sun and the wind, glinting like steel, its sky pierced by maguey spikes.

The melting-pot aesthetic, dressed in the finery of Manhattan and Beverly Hills, has infiltrated the trendy elites of Europe, bringing with it the double token of exoticism (Mexico, tequila) to be enthusiastically downed in the fashionable bars and cafés of Neuilly and Les Marais as though the drink and the country were one and the same.

Meanwhile, the Mexico that foreigners saw—the Mexico of Eisenstein, Artaud, Lawrence, Breton, Lowry, Traven, Bowles or Burroughs—has implanted in a cultured and cosmopolitan international public the specter of a sedate and arcane country, a breeding ground for paradox, ruled by invincible forces; the birthplace of great civilizations which surface in powerful and enigmatic layers. In association with this image, tequila is seen as the liquor of an ancient land, the refinement of gentlemen, a potion of occult wisdom which the seeker takes in order to venture (through an exploration of the tongue and of the veins) into the mythical land of the five suns.

More prosaically, it came to pass that members of the Mexican urban middle class were blessed with an unexpected and priceless gift. Sometime in 1982, many drinkers who could no longer afford their second-rate Scotch, insipid but imported wines and extravagant cocktails, discovered a forgotten treasure on their shelves:

Francisco Gálvez.
The Deer Hunt. 1872.
Oil on canvas.
28 3/4 x 37 in.
Collection of M. Claudio Jiménez.

magnificent bottles of tequila which *malinchismo*—or the infatuation with everything foreign—had forbidden them to enjoy.

The hoary past of this now venerable monument (unveiled by José María Muriá) has been clandestine and evangelistic, liberal and distinguished. Each of its ages is written into its substance and its signs.

The tongue recognizes sensations, the brain, meanings: taste is the meeting of the two. We know what tequila and its name taste like. We can only conjecture what they know: what lingers in the memory of maguey, from whose body emerged—as María Palomar has noted—the paper for certain codices and the cloak called *ayate*.

Besides its subtleties and its warmth, tequila is also the vehicle of images and myths, the faithful witness of a generous world. To approach it is to savor some of the finest things remaining of that universe of the country gentlemen, spawned by a land where time still unfolds like a plant, and where men have not relinquished the privilege of watching the sunrise on horseback, and listening to nightfall from a leather chair on the verandah.
Translated by Lorna Scott Fox.

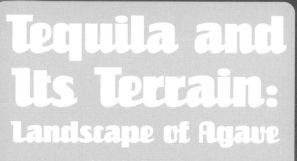

Tequila and Its Terrain: Landscape of Agave

Landscape of Agave

María Palomar

In memory of Antonio Gómez Robledo,
eminence and depth.

What kind of eccentric landscape gave birth to the mezcal from Tequila, the "wine of the earth," from this peripheral region of western Mexico? What was the origin of this hybrid— a drink that would become an undisputed national symbol? "In the remotest confines of these West Indies, in its westernmost regions, almost at those very limits which are the frontier of human exchange and trade, it seems that nature tired of extending itself to such rugged and intemperate lands, and did not want to create more of the world. Instead it raised that one piece of earth, left it useless and barren of all human life, at the mercy of the natural elements and the domain of grasses and frightening solitude."

These few lines are all Bernardo de Balbuena had to say about this landscape in the prologue to his work celebrating the native wonders of New Galicia, his adopted home after having been uprooted from the Iberian Peninsula as a child. As the true limit of the Spanish Empire—its western outpost, frontier and wilderness— the landscape of this region has its own peculiar ways of revealing itself as both fierce and generous. (Jagged, dusty hills of undeniable volcanic ancestry, with crags and canyons and mountains that cast shadows as sharply defined as death itself—the place where the western land touches the sea is the image and emblem of a certain Mexican temperament.) It is a vast yellowed cloth that has been somewhat carelessly unfurled: in such even terrain, the folds resemble monstrous scars, overwhelming protuberances that are authentic accidents—of the serious kind.

However, there are footprints on this barren plateau left by the passing of ancient peoples. The offerings placed in their discreet and subterranean tombs bear witness to a

In the remotest confines of these West Indies, in its westernmost regions, almost at those very limits which are the frontier of human exchange and trade, it seems that nature tired of extending itself to such rugged and intemperate lands, and did not want to create more of the world. Instead it raised that one piece of earth, left it useless and barren of all human life, at the mercy of the natural elements and the domain of the grasses and frightening solitude.... Bernardo de Balbuena

refined aesthetic sensibility and certain indications (for example, their early use of metal) speak of a complex civilization that was linked to the rest of Mesoamerica as far as its eastern limits, and perhaps even to cultures of the South American Pacific coast. On the surface, there is little evidence of the passing of these ancient peoples. But on this pristinely wild terrain the same elements that sustained those distant lives have not changed. Among the miniscule marks punctuating this geography we find the agave and the barbed certainty with which its spears conserve the moist source of nutrients. At one time, this plant provided needles and thread, clothing and shelter for the poor, and even paper for indigenous scribes.

The uses of the maguey, that pagan blessing, are dutifully recorded in the codices, the earliest chronicles—the writings of those who first tried to understand the *genus loci* of these regions. The definitive baptism of Christianity would later contribute its own symbols to the collective soul. When the Europeanization that created the colonial spirit gave way to a genuine blending of cultures during the seventeenth century, the waking dream that reconciled the Spanish Empire's Renaissance brand of Christianity with the classical grandeur of the indigenous past was expressed in The Eighth Wonder: the appearance of the Virgin of Guadalupe on a humble cloak of maguey fiber. This miracle on Tepeyac Hill made the most brilliant jewels of the Spanish Crown pale in comparison, according to another New World Spaniard, Jesuit poet Francisco de Castro:

A green satin called maguey
springs from the soil across this blighted region
that is so fruitful to your owner.
It bestows no blue skies on other lands,
and is invulnerable to the attacks of time,
surviving the sun, the rain, the frost;
your winged heart tells of spiked leaves
sharper than Flemish arrows....

The terrain is desolate, the land arid and rocky. Immense fields of maguey signal our proximity to Tequila, the city of mezcal. The sight of those dry and rocky plains covered with thorny plants brings to mind the forgotten circle of Dante's inferno. It is not, however, a cursed land. **Ernest de Vigneaux**

I owe in my style and in my pen
this fame to the Virgin Mother:
the glory of New Spain,
the Ancient one, the root, the weave
of poor cloth that held so much:
a blossoming copy of Jesse's branch;
from fiber to flower, it packed miracles
into this image of the new Guadalupe.

The noble title of the maguey plant has had a long history in the Mexican landscape, though it was not the maguey but the nopal cactus that was consecrated on the Mexican flag, surmounted by the Aztec, Habsburg or centralist eagle. According to María Moliner, the Spanish word *paisaje* (landscape) is linguistically grouped with *pago* which comes from the Latin *pagus* (village) and is the root of the words *país* (country) and *pagano* (pagan). *Paisaje* comes to us from the French word *pays* which means both nation and region—the fatherland and the motherland, respectively. It has had echoes throughout the centuries. Following the same etymology, *paisano* (meaning both *payés*, or peasant, and civilian in the legal sense, not the military one) is *pagano* (lay or secular, not clerical): in other words, it means a being connected to the *pagus* and close to the *genii loci*, who are the primal spirits of the earth.

The landscape of tequila makes a definite impact, but is never revealed in its entirety, and even less so to the eyes of foreigners who doubt the power of tequila and its fierce and hearty rural temperament. The travelers who passed through the region during the nineteenth century left us disparate images and observations. This is the case of the writings of the Italian J. C. Beltrami (whose description was written in 1823) and the Englishman W. H. Hardy (who visited the region only two years later). The first writes, "Although Tequila is a beautiful village, it is surrounded by what seems a barren region to European eyes. However, in Mexico even bad land bears fruit and riches; the maguey and other indigenous plants have provided Tequila with a prosperity that grains will not.... The Tequila maguey produces a high-quality liquor, the liquor that is called mezcal wine." For his part, the British subject affirms, "Three leagues northeast of Guadalajara lies the flourishing town of Tequila, surrounded by gardens and sugar plantations and a type of maguey which is not as large as that grown near Mexico City for making pulque, Mexico's favorite drink. Here, there is no pulque. This smaller maguey plant is fermented and produces a whiskey, which is distilled into a much stronger spirit called *chinguerite*." In 1853, the Frenchman Ernest de Vigneaux narrated his experiences as a prisoner of war being transported through the Tequila region: "The terrain is desolate, the land arid and rocky. Immense fields of maguey signal our proximity to Tequila, the city of mezcal. The sight of those dry and rocky plains covered with thorny plants brings to mind the forgotten circle of Dante's inferno. It is not, however, a cursed land. After banana and corn, whose use is more basic, the American maguey (agave) is the most precious gift nature has bestowed on Mexico."

In 1856, a journalist from California named Merwin Wheat, who wrote under the pen name Cincinnatus, published a series of travel letters. With a mixture of enlightenment and ignorance—and a good measure of infuriating prejudice—he went from Tepic to Guadalajara and described the desertlike appearance of the region before reaching Magdalena (where a lake still existed). Later he wrote, "Something aroused an even greater sense of awe in us: the contemplation of a picturesque backdrop of mountainous landscapes with all the varying formations of cone-shaped and oblique contours that volcanic heat is capable of producing. For a distance of eighteen miles around, one does not notice any specific difference in the general characteristics of the territory. Having said this, I

Something aroused an even greater sense of awe in us: the contemplation of a picturesque backdrop of mountain landscapes with all the varying formations of cone-shaped and oblique contours that volcanic heat is capable of producing. For a distance of eighteen miles around, one does not notice any specific difference in the general characteristics of the territory. Having said this I cannot claim that the panorama is completely monotonous, nor that we simply continued seeing the lake or the valley, but rather that specific changes wrought by the convulsive nature of this region surged into view at every instant. **Cincinnatus**

cannot claim that the panorama is completely monotonous, nor that we simply continued seeing the lake or the valley, but rather that specific changes wrought by the convulsive nature of this region surged into view at every instant." Even these distant and foreign perspectives celebrated the unyielding character and harsh beauty of the landscape of tequila. A land of surprising texture, with changes as abrupt as they are exceptional, western Mexico expresses its vocation for creating solitary plains marked by strong contrasts.

Faithful only to itself, this rugged landscape is unfathomable and fierce in its depths, upright and steadfast in its heights—whether we are speaking of the land or of its people. Despite everything, the children of the conquistadors certainly knew how to appreciate and assimilate the "American Marvel" with its aesthetic of the terrible and its ritual and pagan hostility. These rugged individuals were the product of an early modernity, one that brought the debate over the earth's roundness to a decisive conclusion in the sixteenth century. The modernity of the twentieth century taught us to regain our awareness of the ungrateful beauty of the unknown. It freed us from the perplexity of the Counter-Reformation, and allowed us to submerge ourselves in "primitive" images, untamed landscapes and uncensored, remorseless pagan sensibilities.

Today, there is no doubt that Mexico's imaginary is indebted to André Breton, whose *Souvenir du Mexique* (Memory of Mexico, 1938) provides an emblematic, simple and definitive description of the maguey and its land: "Red earth, virgin earth, impregnated with the most fertile blood, a land where human life has little value, and— like the agave that extends to the horizon—is always prepared to be consumed in a flower of danger and desire." *Translated by Susan Briante.*

II

The Art of Tequila

Álvaro Mutis

Panegyric and Emblem

For María and Juan Palomar

Tequila is a pallid flame that passes through walls

and soars over tile roofs to allay despair.

Tequila is not for men of the sea

as it fogs their instruments of navigation

and disobeys the unspoken orders of the wind.

On the other hand, tequila is pleasing to passengers on trains

and to those who run the locomotives, for it is faithful

and blindly loyal to the parallel delirium of the tracks

and to the brief haven of the stations

where the train stops to testify

to its inscrutable fate: to wander according to unappealable laws.

There are trees in whose shadow it is a delight to drink tequila

with the tranquility of someone who preaches even to the wind

and there are other trees where tequila cannot bear the shade

which eclipses its powers and in whose branches sways a flower

as blue as that proclaimed by vials of poison.

When tequila waves its flags with their jagged edges

the battle grinds to a halt and the armies turn back

to the order they were intending to impose.

Tequila is frequently accompanied by two attendants: salt and lime.

Yet it is always willing to engage in dialogue,

backed by nothing other than its lustrous transparency.

At first, tequila knows no borders.

But certain climates favor it

as do certain times, which it possesses with full authority:

when night comes to pitch its tents,

in the splendor of a midday without obligations,

in the most towering darkness of doubt and confusion.

That is when tequila cheers us with its lesson of consolation,

its infallible pleasure, its frank indulgence.

There are also dishes that demand its presence:

those favored by the land that witnessed its birth.

It would be unimaginable should they not consort with millenary confidence.

To break that pact would be a serious affront to a dogma prescribed

to make lighter the harsh work of living.

If "gin smiles like a dead child,"

tequila watches us with the green eyes of a sentry.

Tequila has no history; there are no anecdotes

confirming its birth. This is how it's been since the beginning

of time, for tequila is a gift from the gods

and they don't tend to offer fables when bestowing favors.

That is the job of mortals, the children of panic and tradition.

Such is tequila and so shall it lead us

unto the silence from which no one returns.

So, blessed may it be, unto the end of our days

and blessed be its daily diligence in resisting that end.

Translated by Mark Schafer.

Journey
into Transparency

Vicente Quirarte

Water of fire, flaming water. Eau-de-vie (aguardiente, firewater) is a liquid that burns the tongue and bursts into flame at the slightest spark. It does not confine itself to dissolving and destroying, as eau-forte does. It vanishes together with what it burns. It is the communion of life and fire. Spirits also provide instant nourishment, filling the hollow breast with their warmth. Gaston Bachelard

For Pedro Cervantes and Jorge Esquinca,
fans of the "horses."

On the first segment of the road joining the cities of Guadalajara and Tequila, there is a convergence of contrasts not unlike the dialogue between thirst and water. The stifling blue sky challenges a land that appears too stubborn to relinquish any of its gifts. In this chromatic combination, the only other hues allowed are those serving to intensify the drama of the encounter. The sky zealously polishes its vaulted ceiling, and the clouds gleam with the brilliance of ivory. The earth is categorical, both in the austerity of drought and with the arrival of the first rains. Depending on the season, it can be clad in subtle shades of ocher, or the deepest greens.

All of a sudden, the landscape is invaded by a new color: a kind of blue that has borrowed only a hint of yellow's potency, and forces a change of mood in us. "Blue is green departing," wrote Elías Nandino, the poet of this land. The laws of time and space have been violated here, as have those of the color spectrum. Green, though inherent to the plant kingdom, has metamorphosed into blue. Like a long-awaited army that surprises us with the magnificence of its weaponry, maguey plants overrun the land where they stand guard over the slumbering tequila. Mathematically perfect in their form, they present arms with a martial precision worthy of the finest warrior race. As befits the younger brothers of the monumental magueys of the Valley of Mexico—to which José María Velasco paid tribute in his canvases—these plants are smaller and more compact. Their pointed, upthrust blades would not welcome a caress. If the intruder had the means to see past this crown of bluish lances, he would discover the massive *piña*, the core of the tequila plant, no less rough and uninviting to the touch. In its spiky, belligerent beauty, this maguey would seem to be warning us of the perils involved when we

Dolores del Río and Emilio "El Indio" Fernández in *Flor Silvestre*. Courtesy of IMCINE.

steal its heart in order to fortify our own. Landscape and labor, man and plant—such are the elements which come together to form the body and soul of tequila. In the words of Agustín Yáñez, "[This is] an activity that roots man to the soil, bound fast by the distant blue of his mezcals scattered through gullies and over hillsides, and makes him surrender to it with as much love and passion as when surrendering to his beloved."

It is hard to believe that a plant of such dour beauty and even overt hostility could be the source of the limpid beverage which has become the emblem of Mexico, both to Mexicans themselves and in the eyes of the world. This being the case, whenever we make tequila a part of ourselves we should reflect on how it contains the history of a culture. The rocky road toward transparency winds through the most intense period of Mexican history, from the late eighteenth century when its inhabitants were seized by the imperious need to belong to an independent nation, to the end of the millennium, by which time tequila had conquered its rightful place in the art, tastes and everyday life of our country.

Turning tequila into a part of ourselves is always—or always should be—a ceremony, a solemn homage to the wise patience of men and a slow, alchemistic transformation. In conjunction with the earth and the landscape, these are the very elements that bring tequila into existence and enable the word to be rolled around the tongue, savoring all the power and the elegance of its three ringing syllables.

Form is substance. Tequila is the town from which the beverage takes its name, and its sound evokes the noble ruggedness of the Mexican Bajío region. Nothing could be more Mexican; by the same token, nothing could be more Mestizo than this particular blend of cultures. The distillation process that crossed an ocean, the maguey whose name the Spaniards found in the Caribbean, the cult of a plant species that provided ancient Mexicans with food, clothing and pleasure—all these elements converge in the history of one of the chief protagonists of our culture. The difficult road to transparency has been traveled for hundreds of years by the beverage we call by its denomination of origin, tequila.

Of all the words we use to denote the foods and drinks which sustain us, none tastes and sounds so much like Mexico as the word tequila. For while Jalisco may be its native land, this is the only one of our beverages to have transcended regional borders and local patterns of consumption, gaining acceptance throughout the country and the world. Smooth and sonorous to pronounce, it contains the first three vowels—two open (E and A) and one closed (I). Each of the three consonants is phonet-

Pages 148–149
Pedro Armendáriz
in *Juan Charrasqueado*, 1947.
Directed by Ernesto Cortázar.
Collection of Pascual Espinoza.

ically distinct: the T is dental, the L liquid and the Q fricative. So when the best time of day finally arrives—in other words, time for the first tequila—the very act of ordering it leaves one's mouth literally watering, and nothing can satisfy its longing except a liquor that is as scorching as it is intense, as cutting and as clear as the glass of the bottle that holds it, as though in a prison without bars.

The word tequila delivers a light rap and a quick harshness in its first two syllables, before softening into the gentleness of the L and the courteous openness of the A—which is also the first vowel uttered by a baby. Finally (as if that were not enough), tequila is the great androgyn of our culture, identifiable with men as readily as with women, for it may be correctly used in both genders: *el tequila* and *la tequila*. In Spanish, champagne is feminine and wine is masculine. Tequila is more commonly masculine, but the women of Jalisco often refer to it in the feminine. There may be a magical explanation for this, if we think of La Tequila as a dangerous sorceress, capable of luring men from hearth and home, inspiring or destroying them, exalting them and leading them to perdition.

The city of Tequila lies at an altitude of 3996 feet above sea level, at a latitude of 20°53'22" north and a longitude of 103°48'51" west. A former Náhuatl settlement, it was originally given the name of Villa de Torre Argas Ulloa y Chávez, on October 16, 1656. The current name, which by extension is that of the most Mexican of spirits, is just over 200 years old, based on the fact that a tequila distilling license was granted to the Cuervo family in 1795.

Edmundo O'Gorman speaks of the invention rather than the discovery of America. In the fascinating case of tequila, one may speak of both at once. An ancient Mexican myth relates the story of Xochitl, the maiden

CASA COLORADA

who discovered the intoxicating honey hidden at the heart of the great pulque maguey. From a ritual standpoint, pulque liquor performed an escapist function— that is, it was a path to the universe of the gods. The fermentation process whereby this and similar beverages are produced is common to many cultures, and in each case, we find the presence of both religious and practical functions. For example, the drink known as *soma* served both purposes for the Hindus. On his fifth voyage, Sinbad the Sailor was captured by a monstrous old man and forced to carry him everywhere on his back. To cheer himself up, Sinbad drank the fermented juice of some fruit. Eventually he gave some to the old man, got him drunk and killed him.

Tequila is so closely linked to our national culture that it has come to embody a wide range of community values and dichotomies: temperance and excess, joy and

sorrow, health and sickness, the celebration of life and the consummation of death. Its physical characteristics, like its powerful sensorial impact, serve to underline this extreme duality: water that is also fire, a diaphanous flame. Certain authors maintain that pre-Hispanic peoples were already familiar with tequila, but the distillation process was in fact unknown to them. Perhaps they attempted to ferment the spiky blue agaves by the same method they used to obtain pulque from maguey. Or a lightning strike could have roasted one of the plants, and someone could have crushed the softened core and extracted the *tepache* juice—the first stage of refinement of a liquid whose objective is to become transparent. Here we should recall an observation made by Bernal Díaz del Castillo, in his *History of the Conquest of New Spain*: "The Indians were feasting with utmost pleasure on maguey leaves that had been seared by a great fire laying waste to the whole region."

Pulque is the drink that has endured the longest as a staple of the Mexican diet. Due to its nutritional qualities, it was even given to children. It used to be more convenient and cheaper than water, especially in view of the low standards of hygiene that prevailed at the time. Tequila has been with us for over 200 years, and made its debut appearance in the imaginary of Mexico and the world around a century ago. A fusion of cultures was necessary for this to happen, enabling a cross between the plant that yielded the *aguamiel*—the sap which was the basis for the whole process—and the distillation method brought to America by the Spaniards, who had acquired it from the indispensable wisdom of Arab culture.

An experienced drinker can easily distinguish mezcal from tequila, but at first their similarities occasioned a number of linguistic confusions, which need to be clarified. Both beverages are baptized by fire, and both strive for a demanding level of transparency. Their processes of production follow similar lines, but they taste quite dif-

The "son" comes from Tecatitlán, and the mariachi from Cocula. The singing is from San Pedro, and the mezcal from Tequila. And Jalisco has the machos, which is why they wear the pants.

Popular Song

ferent, and exert different effects upon the bodies and souls of their devotees. As an example of this confusion, let us quote a traditional song:

The son comes from Tecatitlán,
And the mariachi from Cocula,
The singing is from San Pedro,
And the mezcal from Tequila.
And Jalisco has the machos
Which is why they wear the pants.

In this regionalist hymn of praise, the *vino mezcal* favored by the people of Jalisco must come from the vicinity of Tequila. Etymological and toponymical reference works provide few clues as to the origin of the word; what little we do know provides a synthesis of the world of our so-called national drink. The transparent product squeezed from the heart of the agave was first christened *mexcalli*, from which we derive the modern "mezcal," now used to designate a type of liquor produced and consumed above all in Oaxaca state. Luis Sandoval Godoy has this to add about the origins of the term: "The chroniclers of those days relate that the Mexica people learned early on how to cook the hearts, or *piñas*, of the *mexcalmetl* or magueys, in underground ovens in order to obtain *mexcalli*, from *metl*, 'agave' and *xcalli*, the apheresis of *ixcalli*, 'baked': baked agave or mezcal, a treacly delicacy that exudes a very sweet, natural honey, still sold today in many small-town markets."

Sandoval Godoy also points out that the word agave comes from the Greek *agavós*, "admirable." However, before the two beverages began to be differentiated, tequila used to be known as *vino mezcal* or *mezcal de tequila*, terms which would seem nonsensical today. For mezcal now denotes only the liquor obtained from a type of maguey called *espadín*, which is native to the valley of Tlacolula in Oaxaca. However, during the eighteenth cen-

Pedro Infante
in *El gavilán pollero*, 1950.
Directed by Rogelio A. González.
Collection of Pascual Espinoza.

tury, mezcal signified any alcohol distilled from any species of maguey, since the word could be translated as "baked maguey," this being the second step in the production process.

In an issue of *El Diario de México* from the year 1812, when nationalist insurgency was in full swing, the bounties of this noble fire-water are listed as follows: "Pure mezcal wine has the virtue of being able to cure illnesses, as has been the experience of the inhabitants of those places where the use of the liquor has been permitted. It gently facilitates female menstruation, even increasing its flow as desired, and relieves the pain of childbirth when consumed lukewarm at the onset. It kills worms and prevents other parasites from spreading. Taken at room temperature, it is effective in relieving women's post-natal pains. In order to experience these salubrious effects, the mezcal should be pure, not mixed with water or any other spirit. It is sold from an outbuilding on the same street as the church of the Holy Spirit, between the houses numbered 3 and 4."

As for the origins of one of the most loaded terms in all our emotional and gastronomic vocabulary, we may be enlightened by the words of Jalisco historian, José María Muriá: "Most think the word comes from the Náhuatl *tequitl* (work, duty, job or task) and *tlan* (place), and refers to a site where certain tasks were performed. On the other hand, it could mean 'the place of cutting,' as Jorge Murguía notes in his *Toponimia náhuatl de Jalisco* (Náhuatl Toponymy of Jalisco), from the verb *tequi* which means 'to cut, to work or to toil,' according to Ángel María Garibay Kintana."

The above quotation reveals how nature is apt to imitate art. Either of the suggested etymologies define tequila as an art which requires strength, concentration and site-specificity. The harvester or *jimador*—that specialized executioner, and a key figure in the chain of production—knows just how much he will have to chop, toil and wear himself out in order to extract the heart of the blue agave. One of the most decisive arguments wielded by tequila producers during the 1940s in order to obtain the right to a denomination of origin, was the fact that only the valley of Tequila boasted the optimum climatic and topographic characteristics for the cultivation of *Agave tequilana Weber*, blue variety—the plant of choice for the production of tequila.

The story of the manufacture and distribution of tequila is closely connected to Mexico's political evolution and its fight for freedom. Although Charles II had given royal permission for the production of agave liquor in 1671, the industry was banned in 1785 by Charles III. One fundamental explanation lies in Spain's need to subordinate its colonies by every possible means. It is significant that in 1795, when the Cuervo family was granted its license to make this "country wine," the fifty-third viceroy, Miguel de la Grúa Talamanca y Branciforte, was under

threat by the French colonists of New Spain. Since 1789, France had set her history on a new course, and the prospects for future revolutions in both the Old and New Worlds had been completely altered. Thus the liberation of tequila coincided with the unleashing of social forces committed to the creation of states whose citizens would be equal; with ambitions as egalitarian as the principles established by the initial communion that is tequila.

The most popular alcohol imported from Spain was known as *catalán*. This was a rough aquavit made from grapes that must have resembled modern *orujo*, and it turns up in the literature of the nineteenth century with astonishing frequency. Ironically enough, it was a Catalan—Arnau de Vilanova (1240–1311), a physician, theologian and professor at Lérida University—who invented the still, and first obtained from it a substance which, writes Sandoval Godoy, "he called *esperit de vi*, spirit of wine." In contrast, we find few references to tequila during those years: its social and aesthetic prestige would have to await the next great revolution, that of 1910. We are indebted to José Torrias de Cuéllar for one of the best descriptions ever penned of catalán and its context, showing how the stuff was ingested by drunks, rakes and other misfits of the nineteenth century. The passage is from his novel *Las jamonas*: "Sánchez had gone down to the café, and 'going down' is the appropriate verb, for Sánchez frequented Zúñiga's and Manrique's cafés, as well as the Cazador and the Refugio. In other words, Sánchez had sunk to regularly consuming his one-*real*'s worth of coffee and liquor—a blend known to all the boozy dregs of male society by the name of *fósforo*.

"This potion is a positive milk of misfortune in Mexico, and it weighs heavily in the statistics of public morality as the *guano* which feeds all those half-living brains and half-empty stomachs which form the clientele of the Levite taverns....

"Spleen is the stupidest thing to have when self-medicating this way. The English take tea, followed by a plunge into the Thames or a bullet in the head; in Mexico they opt for *fósforo* to supplement their noodle soup and other comestibles....

"The crockery at these tawdry cafés is anything but refined: there's no point in looking for a delicate Sèvres cup, its rim doubly gilded by the nectar of thinkers; no point in seeking a silver spoon or one by Christoffle, nor the sugar bowl, nor the tongs. No, here they supply the client with a brackish, blackish tincture (tinted by who knows what procedures, or how illegal) in a glass tumbler made in Siete Príncipes street, or in Texcoco; this glass is resting on a white enameled saucer, so chipped that our coffee drinker can ascertain the nature of its raw material; four lumps of sugar lie there on the tray,

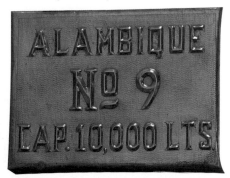

Compañia

Sociedad
CONST
POR ESCRITURAS OT

Coa, a hoe
used for cutting
agave leaves.

whose colors have permanently faded; next to it, the inevitable tin spoon, formed by one snap of a smith's fingers. And in order to save on crockery, while simplifying the whole enterprise, the shot of catalán is already inside the glass into which the waiter slops the coffee. This complex display of uncouthness is what we mean when we speak of *fósforo*."

The clandestine production of tequila began as a reaction against the monopolies of Spain, and also, surely, as the expression of a nascent nationalism. Humboldt remarked on the fact that "*mexical* is forbidden, for to consume it would hurt the trade in Spanish liquors." While the allusions to tequila in nineteenth-century sources are extremely rare, there is an invaluable description by Aniceto Ortega of one distillery of *vino mezcal*, cited by Manuel Payno in his book *Memoria sobre el maguey mexicano y sus diversos productos*: "[The factory] is equipped with vats, sinks or hides for fermentation, a burner for the still, an oven to roast the mezcal, a storeroom and offices. The first step is to establish a number of *quiebras*, that is, to prepare a considerable quantity of magueys, removing the hearts and letting them sit for a fortnight. Then they are scraped, as though to make pulque, and once a day milked of their sap or *aguamiel*, which is left to ferment in the vats, with the help of an astringent plant. The roots of two species of *Mimosa* (*huizachi* and *mezquite*, the acacia of the Nile) may also be used as astringents. These recipients full of aguamiel and *Mimosa* are called pulque containers.

"Meanwhile, all the agave plants that have already been pruned of their *quiote* or castrated, along with some others that are good and ripe, are successively uprooted from the ground. Once their leaves are removed (an operation known as *desvirar*), the exposed core becomes a *piña*, a head of raw maguey or mezcal, and it is transported to the factory and placed in an oven similar to the kilns used for baking bricks or limestone.

"When the oven is full, a fire is lit in the lower part, and once it is burning brightly, the opening is blocked with agave leaves and earth, so as to avoid any heat loss. This system is highly economical with respect to fuel, for as soon as the logs catch fire, the workers begin blocking the upper part with agave leaves, and when the heat reaches that part, they promptly shovel earth over the whole thing, so the mezcal remains insulated for as long as it takes to bake it through and through.

"After this the cooked hearts are taken to the crusher, where they are broken up, mashed and squeezed by a variety of imperfect methods. The most common approach is to beat the material with huge wooden clubs, before trampling it to release the juice.

"The juice obtained, along with the pulp of crushed fibers, or *bagazo*, is put into the vats in a set proportion to the pulque: this forms the liquid to be fermented. The fibers are useful for covering the surface of the mixture in the vats, otherwise much of the brew would be lost to spontaneous evaporation. Furthermore, any traces of juice still trapped in the fibrous mesh also begin to ferment, increasing the final yield. This juice is what gives to mezcal wine its unique flavor, reminiscent of and sometimes identical to Holland gin. Any improvements that diminish this peculiar flavor are rejected by both makers and consumers.

"Once the fermentation is complete, as may be noted by a drop in the level of foam and *bagazo* on the surface (the *caída de montera*, or "fall in the rise," as the specialists call this stage), the mixture is distilled through some very inadequate stills, which allow a considerable leakage of alcoholic vapor.

"The first substance obtained, dubbed *vino ordinario* (ordinary liquor), undergoes a second distillation to produce *vino refino* (refined liquor) which is marketed commercially with an alcohol content of forty-six percent. The initial batches subjected to this second distillation are labeled first flower, second flower, and so on. One wine is rectified by the addition of the *gallina* plant and I don't recall what other less than volatile ingredients; they call it *vino de pechuga*, 'breast wine,' and it is only prepared as a gift."

Most of the leading tequila companies have preserved one factory in the style of those nineteenth-century tequila distilleries. No writer knows more about alcoholic beverages than Manuel Payno. His talent was only matched by his gastronomic knowledge, and on this basis, he turned *Los bandidos de Río Frío* (The Cold River Bandits) into the definitive inventory of nineteenth-century customs, in which the topic of food and drink held pride of place.

Like coffee and love, tequila is irresistible, demanding and powerful. Like coffee and love, tequila is not for the half-hearted. With all its purity, immediacy and vertigo, its highest favors are reserved for those who accept it as part of them. Product of the most refined alchemies— like coffee and love, as well—it is a drink for the initiated, a test for distinguishing appearance from reality. Tequila tastes like its name. Unlike the sweet *xtabentún* of the Southeast, or the smooth *charanda* of Michoacán, the word "tequila" evokes the sound of a bullroarer, the snort of the stallion ridden by a horseman abducting a woman who sells chia-water during Lent.

Clear, naked and overwhelming, tequila's virile nature, though its name may sound feminine, does not require special temperatures nor complicated rituals. It is always better, nonetheless, to first make it part of our lives through a set of simple, but essential, canons. Just as an umbrella should be black and a woman lovely, a *caballito* (a tall shot glass, literally, a "pony") should be tequila's only container and entire continent. Transparent glass to hold the transparency of the tequila. Edgar Allan

Poe (who knew all too well about alcohol) established three requirements for great writing—brevity, intensity and effect. These conditions are summed up in the caballito. When poured by an expert hand, a prime tequila will reward its disciples with a "string of pearls" in a perfect circle along the rim of the glass. The duration of these pearls, as well as their uniformity, depends on the quality and purity of the tequila. The circle of jewels disappears after the first sip, and we can now see that the liquid caresses the walls of the glass, clinging to them like burning lips, as if to say, "Forget me not." We owe one of the best descriptions of this perfect container for tequila to Efraín Huerta, whose thirst was as powerful as his poetry, and who dedicated an entire poem to the caballito, the "David" of the family of glasses: small, powerful and efficient.

In the wee hours of June 15, 1988, the people of Jerez celebrated the centennial of Ramón López Velarde's birth with drums and stiff drinks of mezcal from Zacatecas, served in jugs that the guests hung around their necks with ribbons. While this was practical for their wanderings that evening, it was hardly conducive to savoring the drink. Like my mentor, Efraín Huerta, I confess my ignorance as to why the tequila glass is called a "pony." Gonzalo Celorio interprets the name as a tribute to the measured, galloping ritual that tequila demands of its riders. We use the diminutive form—caballito instead of caballo. We say "caballito" perhaps because the illuminating properties of tequila allow us to trot pleasantly along—and should its noble nature be brutally ignored and its full force unleashed, it would carry us toward the abyss. A steady, processional rhythm is the golden rule for the true connoisseur. As tequila was made for the righteous to savor, it was also made for the stupefaction of those who toss it off with no awareness of what they are drinking. The legions of barbarians from the north, invading Mexico year after year, have exemplified this

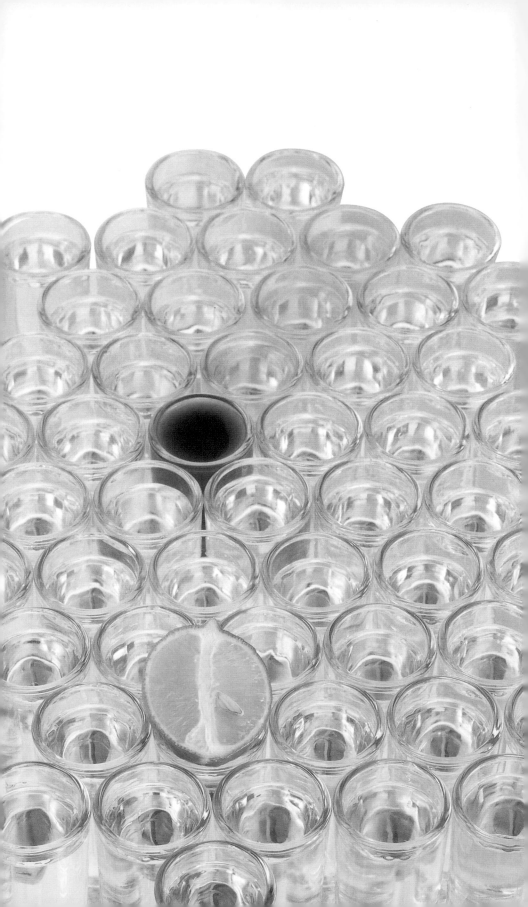

very well with their "tequila shots." Being ignobly possessed by the drink without ever truly possessing it can be roughly compared to the paid favors of eager adolescent sex.

Since the day tequila suddenly became a drink of refined taste, there have been certain unorthodox waiters who believe that they are doing you a great service by pouring it into a brandy snifter. Tequila should breathe in the tall shot glass, *ma non troppo*, as if to embody the transparency referred to in *Muerte sin fin* (Endless Death) by the great Mexican poet José Gorostiza. An unexpected pleasure, on the other hand, was provided to me by a waiter in Santiago, Nuevo León, who asked me if I would like a banderita, or tequila "flag." This consisted of three caballitos, arranged in rigorous chromatic order according to our national color scheme: green lime juice, white—actually, transparent—pure tequila and a shot of red *sangrita* (a blend of spiced citrus or tomato juices).

Where if not in Jalisco? In the La Fuente cantina, near the equally venerable Teatro Degollado, generally one brand of tequila, Centinela, is served in tall shot glasses whose generous height should become the standard, far removed from the finger-measuring stinginess of some bartenders. With one of such glasses, the heart is set aflame; with two, one is carried to the cloud where Lucha Reyes sings *La Tequilera*, the song composed especially for her by Alfredo d'Orsay:

They call me the Tequilera
As if it were my name,
Because that's how they baptized me,
In tequila I was bathed.

Perhaps on account of the generous proportions of the caballitos at La Fuente, Ana Mérida gave what was likely her last public performance. A woman of almost seventy illustrious years, she ignored the complaints of her limbs, as well as the counsel of prudence. Fueled by of seven shots of tequila—a Jaliscan blood transfusion—the tenor who sang *Granada* could not resist the urge to throw herself into the ring once again, seeking to regain the youth that Diego Rivera had captured on the canvas in his portrait of her entitled *Ana of a Thousand Faces*. Her voice accompanied by piano solemnified the drinking ceremony in the cantina, set indelibly in Guadalajara during the 1940s.

To the same cantina we owe a series of poems, written *in situ* by Miguel Angel Hernández Rubio throughout the course of a single day, entitled *Allá en La Fuente* (At La Fuente). This space changes depending on the people in it. In one of these epiphanies, where the limpidness of the tequila appears to momentarily open the doors of clarity, appears the image of Eva, queen of El Jalisco cantina in San Blas, Nayarit. This image, better known as Our Lady of the Gulfs, drinks tequila from a glass which our linguistic blend calls a *chocomilero* (chocolate-milk glass). The poem reads as follows:

> *In tequila*
> *—that burning oil—*
> *the ice*
> *melting*
> *is a diamond*
> *polished by the light of the moon*
> *or the sun;*
> *and after a long, long, long drink*
> *toward that other perfection:*
> *that glass...*
> *that void.*

In Guadalajara there is a cantina without a name, that nevertheless is called Los Caballazos or El Hipódromo by those who frequent it. The spot is the domain of Caballito Cerrero—the only brand served—which is poured into enormous glasses with crushed ice and the customer's choice of soft drink. Sangrita is more expensive than the soft drinks, perhaps because of the belief that the experienced drinker has no need of a chaser. According to local legend, no one has ever drunk more than two of such glasses, served from behind an eighteen-meter tile bar whose length alone should merit it a spot in the *Guinness Book of World Records*. One important code of honor: anyone who shouts or starts any sort of mayhem is obliged to leave the premises—humble though they are, they maintain the dignified presence of the most exclusive gentlemen's club.

A reading of tequila can be made by looking at its different colorings and consistencies against the light— from the transparency of the blanco or white tequila to the dark honey color of aged tequila. But a tour of various tequila producers allows us to compile an inventory of colors, flags and metaphors where each tequila exhibits its particular character. From the date of its triumphant entry into the halls of fashionable consumption, the makers of the most commercial brands have sought to recover the genealogy of tequila production. While novels and the many *corridos* composed since the first major social revolution of the twentieth century exalted the drink's qualities to convert it into a symbol of liberty, happiness and nationalism, the emblems and names of future tequila companies would also reflect similar values.

Since 1906, when tequila first became available in glass bottles, labels for each brand have become as varied as the names of the distilleries where they are made. We can begin our research into these names by delving into some of the more venerable cantinas of Mexico. In many cases, the maguey depicted on old bottles has thin, sharp leaves. This is not the melancholy maguey of large, drooping leaves from which pulque is extracted, but the smaller, sharper tequila maguey. The *Agave tequi-*

lana Weber, blue variety, for example, appears in triplicate on the Tres Magueyes label, and alongside the piña—the heart of the drink—next to a deer's head on the Cazadores brand. The plant also appears on the exotic Newton brand, probably named for its ability to alter the laws of gravity. The Herradura label pays homage to the *campesino* engaged in decapitating a maguey in order to reveal the heart, which will later be roasted before distillation. The story goes that when various producers of the Herradura brand sought to separate and make their own tequila, they tried to find a symbol that had no relation to the former brand. In this way the equally high-quality Caballito Cerrero was born, whose label depicted an orange colt drawn in so naïve a style that it could be mistaken for a deer or a calf. On the other hand, a more clearly drawn horse appears on the label of the almost unobtainable Siete Leguas. The Sauza family proudly features the year 1873 on their bottles—the year in which Cenobio Sauza bought the La Perseverancia factory, formerly known as La Santa Cruz, as depicted in the mural by Gabriel Flores at the Tequila Sauza plant.

The cruel irony of Augusto Monterroso's fable, in which a diner tries some frog's legs and exclaims, "they taste like chicken," can also be applied to those who attempt to illustrate the excellence of a tequila by likening it to cognac. These are the same people who will tell you that Xochimilco is the "Venice of Mexico," and who prefer to drink tequila disguised in the froth of a margarita. Tequila tastes like tequila, and should burn—again, like love or coffee—so that the body feels what it is ingesting. There are palates that prefer well-aged tequilas or even crème de tequila. As an aperitif or the prelude to a banquet, there is nothing like the delicious, direct impact of a white tequila. For the end of a party, likewise, there is nothing like the sweetness of an aged tequila, whose fame resides in the adjective *reposado*, compensation for the long wait and repose in white oak barrels.

"Clearer than water, stronger than moonshine," is how Domingo Lázaro de Arregui described tequila in his *Descripción de la Nueva Galicia* in 1621. While Cenobio Sauza began exporting tequila to the United States in 1873, three subsequent decades of gentility under Porfirio Díaz favored the consumption of foreign liquors here in Mexico. Even the Mexican symbolist poets exalted the effects—whether real or imaginary—of absinthe and other spirits imported from overseas. It was in this context that tequila played such a prominent literary role in the outbreak of the Mexican Revolution in 1910. In *Los de abajo* (The Underdogs), the first novel written about the revolutionary movement, Mariano Azuela opens the second part of his book with the following paragraph: "Rather than champagne, which sparkled in bubbles and dissolved the light and the candles, Demetrio Macías preferred the clear tequila of Jalisco." In the following pages, Macías's troops are found in the midst of a celebration where they boast of their killings in combat and of the advances achieved during their incursions into the houses and haciendas of the rich. A knowing wink by Azuela establishes the confrontation between two worlds: "Among the crystal, porcelain and flower vases there were numerous bottles of tequila."

Fuel for suicidal attacks by Pancho Villa's Northern Division, tequila is also the companion of sorrow and pleasure. Camila discovers its curative properties when Luis Cervantes uses it to disinfect a wound. The anonymous composer of *La Valentina* compared tequila to another drink that also had its origin in its Spanish name of *jerez*:

> If today I drink tequila
> tomorrow I'll drink sherry
> If you see me drunk today
> tomorrow you'll see me nary.

Tequila is a barometer of social pretension. The Revolution, though triumphant, would quickly forget its nationalistic fervor, turning its eyes once again to the pomp and pageantry of the Porfirio Díaz era. Victoriano Huerta, for example, was a voracious cognac drinker, and Hennessy whiskey is featured in the adventures and misadventures of the young politicians in Martín Luis Guzmán's *La sombra del caudillo* (The Caudillo's Shadow). With a superhuman dose of tequila, used as an instrument of torture, the kidnappers of the deputy Axkaná González warn us in a far more effective manner than any other kind of message—whether subliminal or otherwise—as to the dangers of excess: "Axkaná felt as if he had fire in his mouth, in his throat, in his chest; despite everything that had happened, he was flooded with a sense of immense well-being. Two more gulps, given to him immediately, provoked almost no resistance: they entered him as does a drug which alleviates and frees the body from pain. But this did not last for long; moments later the sensations changed suddenly. He now felt the rapid signs of a terrible drunkenness coming on, a strange intoxication which filled him with a sense not of dizziness, but of drowning. He began to feel like someone else, second by second; a profound change which gathered momentum each time his arteries swelled under the pressure of his blood." In the end, however, the Revolution was unable to impose tequila as the nation's drink. The poet Ramón López Velarde's friends, when baptizing his career as a newsman, did it with a bottle of cognac. And in his novel *Las batallas en el desierto* (Battles in the Desert), set at the beginning of Miguel Alemán's presidency, José Emilio Pacheco emphasized the middle class's desire for foreign drinks and its tendency to "whitewash Mexican tastes."

Gilberto Owen was, among other things, the alcoholic conscience of the group known as Los Contemporáneos. He left Mexico in 1928 and returned in 1943. The country and its capital had changed drastically, and

Owen made three discoveries that moved him: the El Nacional building, his eighteen-year-old niece, and tequila. In Bogotá, where Owen had been married to a Colombian woman, he would begin drinking the local liquor of Cundinamarca early in the day; it was served to him in a teacup so as not to scandalize café society. Back in Mexico City, living on the Calle de Mesones, Owen would frequently interrupt his notes and translations to have a few tequilas at the Salón de los Espejos, which still exists. For him, the drink was a kind of reinstatement into his homeland, "a secure anchor and a farewell to adventure," as Owen called alcohol, the metaphoric fuel for the voyage of his character, Sinbad the Stranded.

Cantinflas, the famous Mexican comedian, also owed some of his more memorable scenes to tequila. Under the direction of Arcady Boytler in the film *¿Águila o sol?* (Heads or Tails, 1937), Cantinflas and Medel engage in some of their finest acting when—as any self-respecting Mexican would do—they attempt to drink just one more tequila before retiring. Their tequila-fogged spree, however, has brought the two friends to such a fascinating conversation, such a tight embrace, that they keep bumping their heads together. One-sided speeches, canonical phrases, in which each attempts to construct his own discourse and respond to the other's, are the verbal instruments orchestrated by the little glass of tequila which becomes the key to the wild release of affinities, wounds and passions.

A blanket for the poor, a shield for those who have been abandoned, tequila is noble, transparent and sober (oxymoron notwithstanding). One of the finest tributes paid to the triangle formed by man, woman and tequila was by a poet whose name I will never remember. For several months straight, he religiously bought a half-pint of Hornitos tequila every night—it was all he could afford—and drank it in measured sips on the sidewalk in front of the house of his lost love, without her being able to look at him and with no other compa-

Mario "Cantinflas" Moreno
and Manuel Medel
in *¿Aguila o Sol?* 1937.
Directed by Arcady Boytler.
Courtesy of IMCINE.

ny but the flame of the "lightning bolt that never dies" as it cauterized his wound. Later, without knocking at the door, he would continue on his dark way, lit only by the noblest product of the agave.

"The Ibargüengoitia hour" was Joy Laville's name for that time of day when her husband would interrupt his work to watch the young girls as they left school for home. The great writer and playwright would always accompany the ritual with a glass of tequila as fleeting and intense as the girls' beauty and nimbleness. In Jorge Ibargüengoitia's luminous shadow, it is possible to conclude that the true devotee of tequila begins to take on the liquor's noblest qualities. By its light, the shadows recede, the landscape brightens, and we become as diaphanous as the drink which, stride by stride, becomes a part of us. With its benign hangover, its lengthy stay in the body, tequila was born to accompany our best adventures, which are always journeys within the soul. "My soul is always a little drunk with tequila," sings Lucha Reyes as if to teach us that the spirit reigns over all our deeds. *Translated by Lorna Scott Fox and John T. O'Brien.*

Miraculous Tequila

Chole is the one to blame for my misfortune. Say what they may, Apolonio is innocent. It's just that nobody understands him. If he beat me from time to time, it was only because I made him lose his patience, and not because he was cruel. He always loved me. He loved me in his own way— but he loved me. No one will ever convince me otherwise. If he went out of his way to get me to accept his lover, it was because he loved me. He didn't have to tell me about her. He could have kept her a secret, but he says he was afraid I would find out about his affairs and leave him. And he couldn't bear the thought of losing me, because I was the only one who understood him. My neighbors can preach all they want, but just how many of their husbands tell them about all the women they have on the side? Not one of them. No, the only honest man is my Apolonio. He's the only one who cares for me. The only one who worries about me. With this AIDS thing, it's really dangerous for a man to go hopping from bed to bed, so instead of having a lot of women, he decided to make a sacrifice by taking on just one full-time lover. This way I was at no risk of getting the disease. And that's no bullshit! That's real love. But what do they know!

I have to admit that in the beginning it was even a little hard for me to understand. In fact at first I even said "no" to the whole thing. Adela, my best friend's daughter, was much younger, and I was scared that Apolonio would go and leave me for her. But my "Apo" convinced me that this would never happen. He said Adela meant nothing to him. It was just that he needed to make the most of the last few years of an active sex life, that it was now or never.

I asked him why he didn't make the most of it with me, and he explained it thoroughly to me until I agreed that it was out of the question where the two of us were concerned. To sleep with me would be pointless since I was his wife, and he could have me whenever he wanted. He needed to prove he could seduce younger women—one of those male things that we women can't understand. If he didn't prove it to himself, he'd lose all his confidence, develop hang-ups and be incapable of ever fulfilling his duties as a husband again. Now that really scared me. I told him it was all right and accepted the fact of him having a lover. So I went with him to talk it over with her, because Adelita, whom I had known since she was a child, was extremely embarrassed, and she wanted to hear it from my own mouth, that I had given her my permission to be Apolonio's lover. She explained that she didn't want to settle down with Apolonio. She just wanted to help our marriage and said it was better for Apolonio to see her, not some other tramp who might really want to take him away from me. I was grateful for her thoughtfulness, and I think I even gave her my blessing. The truth is that I was more than grateful, since she was also making a sacrifice for me. As young as she was, Adela could have married and had kids, but instead she was willing to be Apolonio's full-time lover, just because she's a nice person.

Well, that day we had a good long talk and straightened things out between the two of us: the schedule, the days he would visit her, and so on. Under the circumstances, I should have felt fine. Everything was under control. Apolonio was going to settle down and all was wool and a yard wide. But for some reason I was miserable.

When I knew that Apolonio was with Adela, I couldn't sleep. I spent all night imagining what they were doing.

Pages 184–185
Delia Magaña, "La Guayaba,"
and Amelia Whilhelmy, "La Tostada,"
in *Nosotros los pobres*, 1947.
Directed by Ismael Rodríguez.
Courtesy of Cineteca Nacional.

Well, it didn't take much imagination to figure that out. I knew what they were doing, period. And I couldn't help being tormented by it. The worst part was trying to play the happy wife peacefully asleep, since I didn't want to make my "Apo" angry. He didn't deserve that. One day he came in and found me awake. He was furious. He called me an emotional blackmailer and demanded to know why I couldn't let him have a good time without me spoiling it for him. How could he give me any more proof of his love? And yet how did I repay him? By spying on him, by tormenting him with my misty eyes and fears that he was never going to come back. Had he ever missed even a single night? And it was true. Though he got in at five or six in the morning, he always came home. I had nothing to worry about. I should have been happier than ever, yet—God knows why—I wasn't. What's worse is that I started to get sick, I was so mad at that bastard Apolonio. It made me angry to see that he bought Adela things he had never given me. He took her out dancing, when he never took me out. Not even on my birthday when Celia Cruz was singing and I begged him to take me. Out of sheer anger, my eyes started turning yellow, my stomach bloated, my breath soured, my eyes burned and my skin became blotchy.

It was then that Chole told me that the best remedy in such cases was to submerge a handful of boldo tea leaves in a liter of tequila, and have a cup of it in the morning before breakfast. Tequila with boldo absorbs bile and rids the body of anger. Well, I didn't need to be told twice to go to the corner store. I bought a bottle of tequila from Don Pedro and prepared it with the boldo tea. The next morning I drank it, and it worked. Not only did I feel cured, but I was happier than I had been in ages. After a while, the effects of the remedy were even stronger. Seeing that I was calm and smiling all the time, Apolonio began to visit Adela more often, which was all I needed to pour myself a little drink, regardless of what time of day it was, so that the surge of bile would do me no harm. My visits to Don Pedro's store became more and more imperative. A bottle of tequila, which at first had lasted me a month, now barely lasted a single day. Sure enough, though, there wasn't a drop of bile in my body! I felt so good I started to believe that tequila with boldo had miraculous healing properties. It went down my throat cleansing, invigorating, healing, comforting and warming my entire body—making me feel alive, alive, alive!

The day Don Pedro said he could no longer give me credit, not even for one more bottle, I thought I would die. I knew I couldn't make it through the day without my tequila. I begged him. Seeing how desperate I was, he took pity on me and agreed to let me pay in kind. Well, I guess I always knew that deep down inside I was no good. The honest-to-God truth is that with so much heat surging through my body I was willing to do anything, and it was there on the counter that Apolonio found us, giving free rein to our desires. Apolonio has since left me for being a drunk and a whore. He now lives with Adela. I've since led a life of ruin. And all on account of that bitch Chole and her remedies! *Translated by John T. O'Brien.*

Efraín Huerta

To Help Hildebrando Pérez Learn to Drink a Shot of Tequila

Your left hand drawn taut. Ready? Now watch: on the back,
between the thumb and index finger, a hollow, a slight hollow
like a grave dug by none other than God in all His splendor.
The white tequila has been poured into the tall shot glass.
I've never found out why it's called a pony;
perhaps because after five shots one begins
to gallop over sea and sky on the mare Siete Leguas,
for you should know that the horse Siete Leguas
—"Siete Leguas was the horse that Villa loved most of all,
for he would rear and whinny every time the trains would call"—
was no horse at all but a mare as hot as can be, like,
say, the renowned Valentina or the notorious Adelita
or some Peruvian or Mexican poetess at home in her milieu.
All right, now in the little hole (if you have one) on the back
of your taut left hand, a small heap of salt. Got it, brother?
Bring your hand toward your eager mouth, approximately
twenty centimeters, give or take a few: open your mouth
and with your right hand slap the stiff fingers
of your left hand: the salt heap leaps mouthward
and the ritual begins. Suck on a lime. Drink.
A caballito is good for five or six nips.

If you have no hole on the back of your left hand, that is—
then drink as they did in days gone by: squeeze the lime into the glass
add the salt—and you're set.
It's a shame that in your Limaperú you have no
sangrita (tomato juice, very special)
made by a widow born and bred in Jalisco, very tapatía,
to soften the hard gulp of tequila.

In any case, one way or another, the moment will arrive
when you earn your bachelor's,
—never a doctorate—
as an authentic, true-blooded Mexican cowboy,
which is almost like attaining a certain standing
as a hypocritical drinker.

Translated by Mark Schafer.

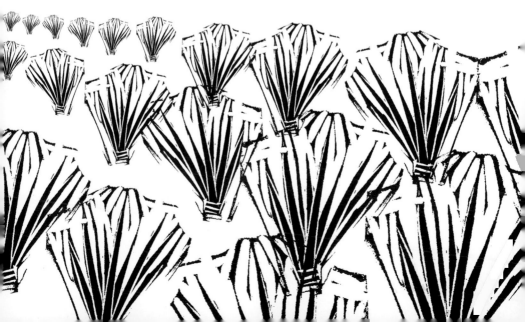

III

Recipes with Tequila

Recipes
with Tequila

Juana Lomelí

Cocktails

Margarita

2 ounces blanco tequila, 1 ounce Cointreau,
the juice of 2 limes, ice, salt
Moisten the rim of a cocktail glass with lime juice and dip in a saucer full of salt until coated. Pour tequila, Cointreau and lime juice into a cocktail shaker with crushed ice and shake. Serve in prepared glass.

Mexican Rose Margarita

2 ounces blanco tequila, 2 ounces Cointreau,
1 red pomegranate, the juice of 2 limes, ice, salt
Coat the rim of a cocktail glass with lime and salt as for a margarita. Cut pomegranate in half and juice with an orange juicer. Pour into a cocktail shaker along with tequila, Cointreau, lime juice and ice, and shake. Serve in prepared glass.

Bloody María

2 ounces blanco tequila, tomato or clamato juice, juice of 1 lime,
1/2 teaspoon Tabasco sauce, 1/2 teaspoon Maggi or soya sauce,
1/2 teaspoon Worcestershire sauce, ground black pepper to taste,
ice, 1 celery stalk
Combine the tequila, lime juice, sauces and pepper. Serve over ice in a highball glass. Add tomato or clamato juice to fill glass, stir, and garnish with the celery stalk.

Tequila Caipirinha

2 ounces tequila, 2 limes, 2 tablespoons sugar, ice
Halve limes and remove seeds. Crush whole limes with sugar and tequila in a mortar. Serve over ice in an old-fashioned glass.

Tequila Sunrise

1 ounce blanco tequila, 1/2 cup orange juice,
1 ounce grenadine, ice
Combine tequila and orange juice. Pour over ice in a highball glass. Add grenadine slowly and serve without stirring, with a swizzle stick.

Charro Negro

2 ounces tequila, cola, ice
Serve tequila and cola over ice in a highball glass.

Pages 194–195
Elena Climent. *Still Life*. 1994.
Watercolor. 7 X 10 1/4 in.
All the illustrations in this
section are by Elena Climent.

Fruit Toritos

2 ounces blanco or reposado tequila fruit beverage, ice
In an old-fashioned or highball glass, serve tequila and the fruit beverage of your choice over ice. (Recipes for fruit beverages follow.)

Limeade with Spearmint

3 limes, 4 sprigs fresh mint, 5 tablespoons sugar,
4 cups purified drinking water
Quarter limes and remove seeds. Purée in blender with remaining ingredients. Strain immediately and refrigerate.

Prickly Pear Drink

10 prickly pears, 1 lime, 5 tablespoons sugar,
6 cups purified drinking water
Halve lime and remove seeds. Peel prickly pears. Place all ingredients in blender and blend thoroughly. Strain and refrigerate.

Citronade

3 citrons, 5 tablespoons sugar,
4 cups purified drinking water
Wash and quarter citrons and remove seeds. Purée all ingredients in blender, strain and refrigerate.

Soursop Drink

1 medium-sized ripe soursop (guanábana), 6 tablespoons sugar,
6 cups purified drinking water
Carefully peel and seed the soursop. Purée all ingredients in blender and refrigerate.

Sangrita

2 cups orange juice, 4 tablespoons catsup,
2 tablespoons Maggi or soya sauce, 2 tablespoons Worcestershire
sauce, 1 tablespoon Tabasco sauce, the juice of 2 limes
Combine all ingredients and refrigerate. Serve well-chilled as a tequila chaser.

Green Sangrita

1 cup orange juice (preferably from green oranges),
the juice of 2 limes, 4 sprigs fresh mint, 3 sprigs fresh cilantro,
4 green serrano chili peppers, 1 teaspoon sugar, salt to taste
Wash mint and cilantro. Remove mint leaves from stems and discard stems. Purée all ingredients in blender and refrigerate until well-chilled. Serve as a tequila chaser.

Soups

Red Gazpacho

4 cups defatted chicken stock, 10 Roma tomatoes,
1 red bell pepper, 2 cloves garlic, 1/2 cup tequila, salt to taste,
1 cucumber, 2 celery stalks, croutons
Seed and de-vein red pepper. In a blender, thoroughly purée tomatoes, red bell pepper and garlic along with tequila, chicken stock and salt. Serve well-chilled with chopped cucumber and celery, garnishing with croutons just before serving.

Green Gazpacho

4 cups defatted chicken stock, 8 green tomatillos,
1 cup fresh parsley leaves, 1/2 cup fresh mint leaves,
1/2 chopped onion, 1 clove garlic, 1/2 cup tequila, salt and pepper
to taste, 1 cucumber, 1 green bell pepper, corn tortillas
Cut tortillas into strips and fry lightly until golden; set aside. Remove outer leaves from tomatillos and wash. Blend chicken stock, tomatillos, parsley, mint, onion, garlic and tequila thoroughly in blender. Season with salt and pepper. Refrigerate and serve with chopped cucumber and green bell pepper, garnished with tortilla strips.

Green Borscht

6 cups defatted chicken stock, 1 pound Swiss chard,
3 hard-boiled eggs, 1 onion, 1/2 cup tequila,
salt and pepper to taste

Wash chard and cut into strips. Heat the stock in a pot. When it reaches boiling point, add the chard, remove pot from heat and let sit until chard is cooked. Add chopped hard-boiled eggs, minced onion and tequila. Season with salt and pepper and refrigerate. Serve at room temperature.

Seafood Soup

1/2 pound medium-sized shrimp, 1/2 pound squid,
1/2 pound mussels, 1/2 pound white clams, 3/4 pound red snapper
or sea bass or salmon, 1 fish head, 5 Roma tomatoes, 1 onion,
5 cloves garlic, 1 bouquet garni, 4 tablespoons fresh cilantro,
1/2 cup reposado tequila, olive oil, salt to taste

Remove heads and shells from shrimp and place into a deep pot with 8 cups water. Set cleaned shrimp aside. Wash fish head and add to pot. Add 1/2 onion, 2 garlic cloves, bouquet garni and salt, and cook until it forms a broth. Strain and set aside. Remove pen and viscera from the squid and discard. Slice squid into rings. Cut fish into pieces. Chop tomatoes, the remaining 1/2 onion and 3 cloves of garlic, and sauté in olive oil in a separate pot. Add broth and bring to a boil. Let boil 10 minutes, then add shrimp, squid, mussels, clams and fish. Lower heat and boil 5 more minutes. Add tequila and cilantro, remove from heat and serve.

Main Dishes

Red Snapper with Greens

1 red snapper about 3 1/2 pounds, 8 green tomatillos, 8 green
onions, 6 green serrano chili peppers, 1 bunch fresh cilantro,
1 bunch fresh parsley, 1/4 cup butter, 2 tablespoons olive oil,
1 cup blanco tequila, 2 teaspoons white pepper, salt to taste

Preheat oven to 350°F. Place the whole, cleaned red snapper into a baking dish and cover with butter, salt and pepper. Remove outer leaves from tomatillos and discard; wash and chop tomatillos. Slice green onions lengthwise; chop chili peppers and fresh herbs. Top fish with prepared vegetables. Pour the tequila and olive oil over the fish, cover with aluminum foil and bake 45 minutes or until cooked through. Serve very hot with bread.

Tequila Shrimp

2–2 1/2 pounds medium-sized shrimp, 1/2 cup diced pineapple,
2 dry pasilla chili peppers, 3 cloves garlic,
1 teaspoon grated fresh ginger, 1 tablespoon corn oil,
2 tablespoons butter, 1/4 cup blanco tequila, salt to taste

Split each shrimp nearly through and open in a butterfly. Wash and devein pasilla chilies and cut into strips; mince garlic. Heat the butter and oil in a pan over medium heat. Sauté the pineapple, chilies, garlic and ginger. Place the shrimp cut side down in pan and add salt and tequila. Continue cooking until shrimp is done and serve immediately.

Leg of Lamb with Tequila

1 leg of lamb, 1/4 cup corn oil, 3 tablespoons cider vinegar,
3 cloves garlic, 3 tablespoons crushed black pepper,
2 tablespoons oyster sauce, 4 small onions with green ends,
1 cup reposado or añejo tequila, salt to taste
Grind garlic with oil, vinegar and pepper. Spread this paste on the leg of lamb and marinate one hour. Preheat oven to 350°F. Place lamb on a baking sheet and spread with oyster sauce. Top with chopped green onions and add salt and tequila. Cover with aluminum foil and bake 1 1/2 hours or until cooked through. Serve very hot with *salsa borracha* (chili sauce with pulque) and tortillas.

Tenderloin Fillets in Pepper Sauce

6 beef tenderloin fillets, 3 carrots, 1 red bell pepper, 1 large onion,
2 cloves garlic, 2 cups beef or veal stock, 1/2 stick butter,
1 tablespoon corn oil, 2 tablespoons white wine or vinegar,
1/2 cup reposado tequila, a pinch each of thyme and crushed bay leaves, 1 1/2 tablespoons ground black pepper, salt to taste
Heat butter and oil in a pan. Chop carrots, red pepper, onion and garlic finely and add to pan. Sauté over medium heat until golden. Add the stock and cook at low heat 10 minutes. Add vinegar, tequila, dried herbs, salt and pepper, and continue cooking over low heat until sauce reduces by half. Serve very hot over grilled tenderloin fillets.

Lime Chicken

1 whole chicken about 3 1/2 pounds, 1 cup orange juice,
1/2 cup reposado tequila, 1 whole lime, 2 tablespoons lime juice,
2 tablespoons butter, 2 tablespoons olive oil, 3 cloves garlic,
3 bay leaves, 2 tablespoons coarse ground black pepper, salt to taste
In the blender, make a paste of the garlic and olive oil. Spread this paste over the chicken, covering it entirely, and marinate 1 hour. Preheat oven to 350°F. Place chicken in a baking dish and spread butter over it. Stuff chicken's cavity with the lime cut into quarters and bay leaves. Pour the tequila, orange juice and lime juice over the chicken and sprinkle with pepper. Cover with aluminum foil and bake 45 minutes to an hour, or until cooked through. Remove foil and let brown for another 10 minutes. Serve with white rice.

Desserts.

Josefina Cake

*3 cups sifted flour, 3 cups brown sugar, 3/4 cup unsweetened
cocoa, 1 1/3 cups sour cream, 1 cup butter, 4 eggs,
1 1/3 cups boiling water, 3 teaspoons baking soda,
1/2 teaspoon salt, 2 teaspoons vanilla extract, 1 teaspoon ground
dried chile de árbol (hot chili pepper) 1/2 cup reposado tequila*

Grease and flour a medium round cake pan. Preheat oven
to 300°F. Cream the butter in a large bowl with an electric
mixer. Add the sugar and eggs and continue beating 5 more
minutes. On the lowest speed, beat in the cocoa, baking
soda, vanilla, ground chile de árbol and salt. Gradually add
flour and sour cream, alternating them and mixing until
well combined. Add the hot water and mix with a wooden
spoon. Pour the batter into the cake pan and bake 35 minutes, or until a knife inserted into the center comes out
clean. Cool, remove from the pan and drizzle with tequila;
sprinkle with cocoa.

Orange Loaf

*3 cups sifted flour, 2 cups sugar, 1 cup milk, 1 stick butter,
3 egg yolks, 1 teaspoon baking powder, 1 teaspoon vanilla extract,
1 teaspoon cinnamon, 2 teaspoons grated orange peel,
1 teaspoon grated lime peel, 1/2 cup reposado tequila, icing sugar*

Grease and flour a medium loaf pan. Preheat oven to 350°F.
Cream butter in a large bowl with an electric mixer. Add egg yolks
and sugar and continue beating 5 minutes. Add flour a cup at a
time, mixing well, and then add milk. Add baking powder, vanilla,
cinnamon and grated orange and lime peel. Beat together and
pour batter into pan. Bake 25 to 30 minutes or until a knife inserted into the center comes out clean. Let cool. Remove from pan,
drizzle with tequila and sprinkle with sifted icing sugar.

Tejocotes in Tequila Syrup

*2–2 1/2 pounds tejocotes (haw fruit),
6 cups water, 1 1/2 cups sugar, 1 cinnamon stick,
3 whole cardamom pods, a few strands saffron,
1 1/2 cups reposado tequila*

Cook the fruit in the 6 cups of water and peel. Place the water in
a pot with the sugar, cinnamon, cardamom and saffron and cook
over low heat until it forms a syrup. Add the tequila and fruit and
remove from heat. Pour into sterilized jars and refrigerate.

A Gallery of Tequilas

Allende

This 100% blue agave tequila is manufactured and bottled on-site at the Hacienda Corralejo in Guanajuato, the birthplace of Mexican national hero Miguel Hidalgo. This is why the brand bears the name of his most loyal lieutenant in the fight for Mexico's independence: José Ignacio María de Allende.

Corporación Ansan, S.A. de C.V.
Juan Ruíz de Alarcón 127, Arcos Sur,
44140 Guadalajara, Jalisco.
T. (33) 363 02022 / F. (33) 373 50754
ansan@megared.net.mx

Alteño

The La Quintaneña distillery was founded in 1872 by Francisco Romero González, a pioneer in the manufacture of what was known as "tequila wine" or "mezcal wine" since 1852. That distillery gave rise to Alteño: an exquisite liquor produced with meticulous care using the finest agaves from Los Altos, the region of Jalisco that gave this tequila its name.

Pernod Ricard Mèxico, S.A. de C.V.
José María Morelos 285,
Tequila, Jalisco.
T. (33) 374 20006 / F. (33) 374 20215

Amate

Amate is a traditional handmade paper fabricated by Mexican artisans, and the inspiration for the name of this brand created by Juan Arroyo Rivera and Carlos Monsalve Agraz in Mexico City.

La Cofradía, S.A. de C.V.
Av. de los Novelistas 5063, Jardines Vallarta,
45027 Zapopan, Jalisco.
T. (33) 367 32443 / F. (33) 362 90010
lacofradia@infosel.net.mx

Arfor-Revolución

The first after-dinner digestive tequila. Using a secret process, it is made from the undiluted extract of pure 100% blue agave, and then aged. To avoid confusion with Revolución blanco tequila, the name Arfor was added. Its production process is similar to that of the finest European *eaux de vie*.

205

Milemiglia, S.A. de C.V.
Bosques de Ciruelos 162, Bosques de Chapultepec,
11700 Mexico City
T. (55) 520 37836 / F. (55) 554 52122

Arroyo Negro

Arroyo Negro has emerged as a new choice for those familiar with fine tequila. Its founder, Sergio Goyri, personally oversees its production. The smoothness, sparkling appearance and distinguished quality of this tequila, bottled on-site, confirm that it is a 100% blue agave product.

La Cofradía, S.A. de C.V.
Av. de los Novelistas 5063,
45027 Jardines Vallarta,
Zapopan, Jalisco.
T. (33) 367 32443 / F. (33) 362 90010
lacofradia@infosel.net.mx

Artillero

This 100% blue agave tequila is stored for six months in white oak barrels. The bottle's form is reminiscent of the cannons that defended forts during the colonial era. Its crystal clarity is the result of a careful production process carried out by its creators, the Hernández family.

La Cofradía, S.A. de C.V.
Calle La Cofradía s/n,
46400 Tequila, Jalisco.
T. (33) 367 32443 / F. (33) 367 32492
email: cofradia@mpsnet.com.mx

Canicas

This tequila is elaborated according to time-honored methods in Irapuato, Guanajuato, one of the recognized tequila-production regions specified in Mexican denomination of origin laws. The Mexican marbles (*canicas*) inside its blown-glass bottle simulate the bubbles that characterize a pure tequila and add a touch of originality.

David Partida Zuñiga,
Carretera El Salvador-Amatitlán, Jalisco, km 11,
T. (33) 374 50057 / F. (33) 374 50957

Casa Noble

Stored undisturbed in white oak barrels, this tequila acquires a distinct flavor with a unique personality. Its presentation in an exquisite hand-crafted and individually numbered porcelain decanter with pewter and polished blue ceramic inlays attests to the great creativity of Mexican artisans.

José Ma. Morelos 285,
46400 Tequila, Jalisco.
T. (33) 374 20006
email: tequila@megared.net.mx

Cazadores

Arandas, Jalisco, a land of noble traditions, is where this tequila had its origin, founded by Félix Bañuelos in 1972. It is elaborated in a single style: reposado. It is manufactured according to centuries-old traditions that, in combination with the latest technology, produce this liquor with a generous body.

Carretera Arandas-Tepa km 1,
Arandas Jalisco.
T. (33) 368 64600
email: tevirsa@tequilanet.com.mx

Chinaco

The Chinacos were the most notable and celebrated troops in Mexico since its independence. This tequila was named in honor of their bravery, gallantry and horsemanship. It is made from agaves grown in south-central Tamaulipas, which Mexican denomination of origin laws recognize as a tequila-producing region. The bottle is reminiscent of flasks used by the Spaniards during the colonial era.

Tequilera La Gonzaleña, S.A. de C.V.
Ejército Nacional 404-104, Colonia Polanco,
11570 Mexico City
T. (55) 553 15959 / F. (55) 553 18826
http://www.realtequila.com.chinaco

Comalteco

Comala—the "white town of America"—is the perfect place to sample local delicacies from the state of Colima. The hubbub of its plaza's shaded walks and its mariachi and band music also create the ideal ambience for savoring Comalteco tequila. Its fine quality is the pride of founders Carlos César Romero Moreno and La Cofradía.

La Cofradía, S.A. de C.V.
Av. de los Novelistas 5063, Jardines Vallarta,
45027 Zapopan, Jalisco.
T. (33) 367 32443 / F. (33) 362 90010
lacofradia@infosel.net.mx

Del Terrajal

This tequila pays homage to the bountiful land of Jalisco, where the finest agaves grow and mature. The founders of this brand are four families with a long tradition in Jalisco and a commitment to producing an integral and natural tequila. Its bottle's design and craftsmanship evoke years of sun and rain, patient waiting and the wisdom of experience.

La Cofradía, S.A. de C.V.
Av. de los Novelistas 5063, Jardines Vallarta,
45027 Zapopan, Jalisco.
T. (33) 367 32443 / F. (33) 362 90010
lacofradia@infosel.net.mx

Corralejo

Hacienda Corralejo in Pénjamo, Guanajuato, was the birthplace of Miguel Hidalgo, the founding father of Mexico. The bottle has two engraved crests: one with Hidalgo's signature and the other representing Independence. Bubbles trapped within the glass itself accentuate the bottle's antique appearance and enhance its beauty.

Tequila Corralejo, S.A. de C.V.
Mexico City Offices:
T. (55) 587 70203 / F. (55) 587 70334

Don Tacho

Tacho Ansotegui (Don Tacho) personally oversees the planting and harvesting of excellent agaves in the fields of Valle de Arenal, Jalisco. The refined quality and smoothness of this tequila can also be attributed to its traditional elaboration methods. A nine-month storage period imparts an unusual wood-tinged flavor to the tequila.

Panamericana Abarroteras, S.A. de C.V.
Logo Athabaska 164,
Colonia Huichapan Tacubaya,
11290 Mexico City
Tel. (55) 539 95390
F. (55) 539 91476
dontacho@pasa.com.mx

De los Dorados

This tequila invokes the image of Los Dorados, the notorious and elite armed guard whose members were handpicked by none other than the Centaur of the North: Pancho Villa. Its bottle's label bears a bullethole design and a picture of Villa's troops.

La Cofradía, S.A. de C.V.
Av. de los Novelistas 5063, Jardines Vallarta,
Zapopan, Jalisco.
T. (33) 367 32443 / F. (33) 362 90010
lacofradia@infosel.net.mx

El Jimador

This tequila is patiently stored for three months in white oak barrels, giving it a distinctive personality. The quality of El Jimador reposado pays a well-deserved tribute to the expert fieldworkers who have the responsibility of selecting the best agaves for the Herradura company.

Tequila Herradura, S.A. de C.V.
Av. 16 de Septiembre 635, Zona Centro,
44180 Guadalajara, Jalisco.
T. (33) 394 23900
herraduraventas@infosel.net.mx

Galardón

Specially chosen harvests of the finest agaves are the basis for this tequila. Bottling and labeling is carried out on-site by hand, and each bottle is individually numbered. Its balanced aroma is the result of a patient ten- to twelve-month storage period in fine wood barrels. Ideally suited to serving neat as an aperitif or digestive.

Tequila Sauza, S.A. de C.V.
Av. Vallarta 3273 Colonia Vallarta Poniente,
44100 Guadalajara, Jalisco.
Tel. (33) 367 90600 / F. (33) 367 90693

García

With the founding of the Río de Plata distillery, now Tequilas del Señor, César García initiated a tradition in tequila production that has been carried on by later generations. This brand was created in 1943 in his honor.

Tequilas del Señor, S.A. de C.V.
Río Tuito 1193, Colonia Atlas,
44870 Guadalajara, Jalisco.
T. (33) 365 77877 / F. (33) 365 72936

Goyri

Sergio Goyri was inspired to create this brand after observing the ties between Mexican culture and tequila. Mexican artisans envisioned the bottle's design to symbolize the syncretism of the Spanish and Mexican cultures. It comes in a wooden box with forged iron appliqués.

La Cofradía, S.A. de C.V.
Av. de los Novelistas 5063, Jardines Vallarta.
45027 Zapopan, Jalisco.
T. (33) 367 32443 / F. (33) 362 90010

Herencia de Plata

Manuel García chose this tequila's name to commemorate his children's weddings. Its 100% blue agave purity and traditional elaboration methods create the flavor of the fierce red earth of Los Altos in Jalisco. The blown-glass bottle with its silkscreened label is a fitting container for the "silver legacy" that gave this tequila its name.

Tequilas del Señor, S.A. de C.V.
Río Tuito 1193, Colonia Atlas,
44870 Guadalajara, Jalisco.
T. (33) 365 77877 / F. (33) 365 72936

Farias

To celebrate the hundredth anniversary of the Farias trademark, the heirs of this great tradition—Ricardo Farias I, II and III—decided to initiate the production and distillation of a new tequila, manufactured according to time-honored methods. Its practical bottle in the form of a barrel is designed to guarantee its quality and preservation.

Industrializadora de Agave
San Isidro, S.A. de C.V.
Camino Tepatitlán-San José
de Gracia,
Tepatitlán de Morelos,
Jalisco.
T. / F. (33) 378 22006

Gran Centenario Reserva del Tequilero

This limited-edition tequila is one of the best-kept secrets of the Los Altos region of Jalisco. Gran Centenario Reserva del Tequilero offers a combination of fruity and exotic spicy tastes to the palate, including cinnamon, almond and vanilla. The resulting flavor is pleasant and slightly sweet.

Casa Cuervo, S.A. de C.V
Circunvalación Sur 44-4,
45070 Zapopan, Jalisco.
T. (33) 363 44298 / F. (33) 363 48893

Casa Cuervo, S.A. de C.V
Circunvalación Sur 44-4,
45070 Zapopan, Jalisco.
T. (33) 363 44298
F. (33) 363 48893

Gran Centenario

For over 140 years, the long tradition of quality at Hacienda Los Camichines in Los Altos de Jalisco has motivated its workers to manufacture this tequila with pride. It was in that region, whose red soil is ideal for cultivating *Agave tequilana Weber*, blue variety, that Lázaro Gallardo—master of tequila distillation and the founder of Los Camichines in 1857—discovered the secret to extracting this precious liquid. Time, experience and the type of barrel are the keys to these premium products.

Gran Centenario Azul Gran Reserva

This tequila's manufacture is supervised with utmost care, so its limited availability should come as no surprise. Its deep golden color and exquisite bouquet are due to its lengthy contact with the fine wood of the barrels where it rests undisturbed. It is presented in an elegant and aesthetic blue ceramic bottle.

Casa Cuervo, S.A. de C.V
Circunvalación Sur 44-4,
45070 Zapopan, Jalisco.
T. (33) 363 44298 / F. (33) 363 48893

Herradura Añejo

Created in 1962, this tequila recalls the beauty of the old distillery of the Hacienda de San José del Refugio, a monument to the traditional elaboration and distillation process of tequila. Herradura Añejo acquires its smooth taste over a thirty-month aging period in white oak barrels.

Tequila Herradura, S.A. de C.V.
Av. 16 de Septiembre 635, Zona Centro,
44180 Guadalajara, Jalisco.
T. (33) 394 23900
herraduraventas@infosel.net.mx

Herradura Blanco

This is the oldest tequila in the Herradura family, having originated in 1870 in Amatitán, one of Jalisco's most fertile tequila-producing regions. Its appearance in some of the most celebrated movies from the golden age of Mexican film is testimony to its long tradition and deep roots in our culture.

Tequila Herradura, S.A. de C.V.
Av. 16 de Septiembre 635, Zona Centro,
44180 Guadalajara, Jalisco.
T. (33) 394 23900
herraduraventas@infosel.net.mx

Herradura Blanco Suave

Amatitán, a land blessed for its benign climate, the richness of its soil and the enterprising spirit of its inhabitants, gave rise to this liquor which has been distilled at the Hacienda de San José del Refugio since 1975.

Tequila Herradura, S.A. de C.V.
Av. 16 de Septiembre 635, Zona Centro,
44180 Guadalajara, Jalisco.
T. (33) 394 23900
herraduraventas@infosel.net.mx

José Cuervo Especial

This is the most popular and widely recognized tequila in the world. Fans of this brand enjoy it mixed with cola, orange or grapefruit soft drinks. It is also the key ingredient in millions of margaritas served the world over. This tequila has allowed its producer José Cuervo, initiator of major technological advances in the industry, to achieve a strong international presence.

Casa Cuervo, S.A. de C.V.
Av. Río Churubusco 213, Colonia Granjas México,
08400 Mexico City
T. (55) 580 32400

Herradura Reposado

This was the first reposado tequila ever produced: the legendary Herradura which has been winning over countless connoisseurs around the world since its creation. After thirteen-months' storage, its flavor reaches a perfect balance between agave and wood.

Tequila Herradura, S.A. de C.V.
Av. 16 de Septiembre 635, Zona Centro,
44180 Guadalajara, Jalisco.
T. (33) 394 23900
herraduraventas@infosel.net.mx

Herradura Antiguo

This is a genuine reproduction of the Herradura tequila of 1924 that was served exclusively to the lords of the manor at the Hacienda de San José del Refugio, where Herradura originated. It was not available to the general public back then, but today, Herradura offers the original formula that was held in safekeeping for decades.

Tequila Herradura, S.A. de C.V.
Av. 16 de Septiembre 635, Zona Centro,
44180 Guadalajara, Jalisco.
T. (33) 394 23900
herraduraventas@infosel.net.mx

José Cuervo Añejo

The José Cuervo company takes us by surprise with its most recent presentation, José Cuervo Añejo, a 100% blue agave tequila aged in small white oak casks. Its flavor and its bouquet with a strong woody nose make it the ideal tequila for celebrating any special occasion.

Casa Cuervo, S.A. de C.V.
Av. Río Churubusco 213, Colonia Granjas México,
08400 Mexico City
T. (55) 580 32400

José Cuervo Tradicional

One could say that this tequila had a starring role in the golden age of Mexican film (1940s), appearing alongside such well-known actors as Pedro Infante and Jorge Negrete in countless cantina scenes. Carefully elaborated and genuine, it is the product of José Cuervo's more than two centuries of experience as the world's first tequila company.

Casa Cuervo, S.A. de C.V.
Periférico Sur, 8500,
Tlaquepaque, Jalisco.
T. (33) 363 48586 / F. (33) 363 28081

La Cava del Villano

Created in 1996, this brand evokes the strong ties that exist between tequila and Mexican culture, as reflected by classic scenes in novels and films in which the revolutionary hero drinks this strong liquor in dimly lit small-town plazas or in wild mountain settings. La Cava del Villano is appreciated for its mild flavor.

La Cofradía, S.A. de C.V.
Calle La Cofradía s/n,
46400 Tequila, Jalisco.
T. (33) 367 32443 / F. (33) 367 32492
cofradia@mpsnet.com.mx

La Cofradía

A company with a long tradition in the industry introduced this 100% agave tequila in 1995. It comes from a special reserve and is available in three styles: triple-distilled blanco, six-month-old reposado and one-year añejo. The signature of distillery owner Carlos Hernández Hernández appears on its bottle.

La Cofradía, S.A. de C.V.
Calle La Cofradía s/n,
46400 Tequila, Jalisco.
T. (33) 367 32443 / F. (33) 367 32492
cofradia@mpsnet.com.mx

La Montura

This 100% agave tequila was introduced in 1998 to honor the Mexican charro tradition. The name refers to the typically Mexican emblem of the saddle, which, like the truly national "spirit" of tequila, is symbolic of our culture's Mestizo roots.

La Cofradía, S.A. de C.V.
Calle La Cofradía s/n,
46400 Tequila, Jalisco.
T. (33) 367 32443 / F. (33) 367 32492
cofradia@mpsnet.com.mx

La Perseverancia

A tequila manufactured at the hacienda of the same name, established in Tequila, Jalisco, in 1873. It has a mild character and a fruity flavor that reveals the vegetable origin of the beverage. The bottle's form recalls an agave heart, and allows for easy handling.

Tequila Sauza S.A. de C.V.
Av. Vallarta 3273,
44110 Guadalajara, Jalisco.
T. (33) 367 90600 / F. (33) 367 90693

Los Azulejos

The beautiful design of its cobalt-blue blown-glass bottle was inspired by a pre-Columbian piece from the Mixtec culture. The name draws a link between tequila and Talavera ceramic tiles or *azulejos*—two products of Mexican craftsmanship. After a double distillation, it is stored for four to six months in holm oak barrels.

Agaves Procesados S.A. de C.V.
Amado Nervo 60 BIS, 2do piso,
Colonia San Francisco Fetecala,
02730 Estado de México.
T. (55) 535 24798

Los Arango

Los Arango created this tequila in 1997, and named it after Doroteo Arango, better known as the revolutionary leader Pancho Villa. The blue glass bottle is a fine example of Mexican craftsmanship.

Tequilera Corralejo, S.A. de C.V.
Mexico City Offices.
T. (55) 587 70203 / F. (55) 587 70334

Los Cofrades

This tequila shares the characteristics of refinement and maturity with the *cofrade*, who in the past was a community elder held in high esteem for his wisdom. The Hernández family sought to provide this tequila with a beautiful ceramic bottle that would emphasize the *cofrade*'s staff as an emblem of his high standing.

La Cofradía, S.A. de C.V.
Calle La Cofradía s/n,
46400 Tequila, Jalisco.
T. (33) 367 32443 / F. (33) 367 32492
cofradia@mpsnet.com.mx

Mapilli

Prior to the sixteenth century, the Tecuexe Indians grew *Agave tequilana Weber*, blue variety, in Los Altos of Jalisco. Tribal leader Mapilli negotiated the harmonious union between indigenous knowledge of agave cultivation and the European art of distillation. This tequila was named in honor of this man, a symbol of strength and nobility from the red lands which produce the finest agaves.

Industrializadora de Agave,
San Isidro, S.A. de C.V.
Km 2, Camino Tepatitlán a San José de Gracia,
Tepatitlán de Morelos, Jalisco.
T. (33) 378 22006

Mayorazgo

Even the name Tequila Mayorazgo denotes dominance, superiority and primogeniture, attributes that are reflected in the magnificent presentation of this brand. In 1911, Pedro Velasco Calle founded the La Madrileña company, and in 1970, La Unión distillery was built in Tolotlán, Jalisco—the birthplace of Tequila Mayorazgo. Its quality has won many lifetime converts.

Fábrica de Tequila la Unión,
Distribuldor: La Madrileña, S.A. de C.V.
Arroz 89, Col. Isabel Industrial,
09820 Mexico City
T. (55) 544 51002 / F. (55) 544 51272

Ortigoza

Tequila Ortigoza was created in homage to José Ortigoza, a foreman at Los Magueyes cattle ranch whose dream was to produce his own tequila. His descendents have fulfilled that desire with Ortigoza, a tequila made from 100% *Agave tequilana Weber*, blue variety.

Tequila Sierra Brava, S.A. de C.V.
Aldama 200, El Salvador,
Municipio de Tequila, Jalisco.
T. (33) 362 04583
sierrabrava@prodigy.net.mx

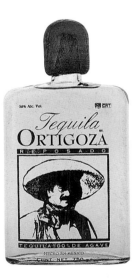

Pueblo Viejo

It all started in 1884 at the San Matías Hacienda in Magdalena, Jalisco. There, Delfino González Chávez distilled a tequila of his own making, exclusively for his own use and to share with his friends. Later, he joined forces with Guillermo Castañeda to build a factory with a freshwater spring. The tradition has been continued by Jesús López Román, who created Pueblo Viejo and San Matías Gran Reserva.

Tequila San Matías de Jalisco, S.A. de C.V.
Calderón de la Barca 177, Arcos Sur,
Guadalajara, Jalisco.
T. (33) 361 50421 / F. (33) 361 61875

Quita Penas

Tequila is said to *quitar las penas*, that is, take away your worries—or at least help you forget them. Quita Penas is produced in Pénjamo, Guanajuato, at the legendary Hacienda Corralejo—a place worth visiting not only to see how this tequila is manufactured but also to discover a part of Mexican history. Founders Javier and Santiago Fernández Gabela gave this tequila an elegant presentation: the cobalt-blue color of its tall, one-liter bottle is reminiscent of the blue agave used in its elaboration.

Tequilera Corralejo, S.A. de C.V.
Carretera San Martín Tepajaco,
km 2 1/2, Colonia San Martín,
54763 Tepatlixpán Cuatitlán Izcalli,
Estado de México.
T. (55) 587 70203 / F. (55) 587 70334

Reserva del Señor

This tequila, founded by the brothers José and Fausto Orendain in the 1940s, is characterized by its refined quality and distinction. Tequilas del Señor acquired the brand in 1986. The bottle's design imitates the shape of a traditional still.

Tequilas del Señor, S.A. de C.V.
Río Tuito 1193,
44870 Guadalajara, Jalisco.
Tel. (33) 365 77877 / Fax. (33) 383 70430

Reserva Antigua 1800
Añejo Reserva 1800 Reposado

These tequilas are products of fine Mexican craftsmanship—a synonym for lineage, elegance and distinction. Its two styles, reposado and añejo, have been the firm's pride since 1800, the year they were created. The añejo tequila is characterized by its woody flavor and bouquet, and by the dark amber hue that distinguishes any aged liquor.

Casa Cuervo, S.A. de C.V.
Periférico Sur 8500,
Tlaquepaque, Jalisco.
T. (33) 363 48586 / F. (33) 363 28081

Reserva de la Familia

Tequila Cuervo celebrated its 200th anniversary in 1995, making it one of the oldest firms in Mexico, as well as the first producer of tequila in the world. To mark the occasion, Cuervo took the family reserves, jealously guarded in its cellars, and made them available to an exclusive clientele. The quality of this tequila can be attributed to the use of only select young agaves. The finely crafted bottle has a label designed at the turn of the century and is presented in a wooden case that features the work of a different artist each year, as a way of making Mexican art known throughout the world.

Casa Cuervo, S.A. de C.V.
Periférico Sur 8500,
Tlaquepaque, Jalisco.
T. (33) 363 48586 / F. (33) 363 28081

Revolución

The name says it all. The 1910 Revolution—an intense episode in Mexican history—provides the backdrop for this tequila made with the finest 100% *Agave tequilana Weber*, blue variety, since 1995. Its presentation is nothing if not deluxe: a 24-karat gold plaque as a label.

Milemiglia, S.A. de C.V.
Bosques de Ciruelos 162,
11700 Bosques de Chapultepec,
T. (55) 520 37836 / F. (55) 554 52122

Sombrero Negro

This tequila evokes the noble men of the rural tequila-producing region, horsemen who found their natural expression in *charrería* and in the transparent warmth of a tequila they recognized as their own. Sombrero Negro has been on the market since the 1940s.

Tequilas del Señor, S.A. de C.V.
Río Tuito 1193,
44870 Guadalajara, Jalisco.
T. (33) 365 77877 / F. (33) 365 72936

Sauza Hornitos

Sauza's admiration and respect for the beauty of Mexican art can be seen in the magnificent murals that adorn the company's buildings, illustrating the birth of this beverage. It was the first 100% blue agave reposado tequila produced by this firm that has 125 years of experience in the industry.

Tequila Sauza, S.A. de C.V.
Av. Vallarta 3273, Colonia Vallarta Poniente,
44110 Guadalajara, Jalisco.
T. (33) 367 90600 / F. (33) 367 90691

Selección Suprema

Selección Suprema is the ultimate expression of the Herradura company. It is aged for five years because only time can take Mexican agave to such a sublime level that tequila may be placed on a par with the finest liquors in the world.

Tequila Herradura, S.A. de C.V.
Av. 16 de Septiembre 635, Zona Centro,
44180 Guadalajara, Jalisco.
T. (33) 394 23900

Sevilla la Villa

This tequila began production in 1998. Its name was chosen to honor Mexico's Mestizo culture. Like the country itself, tequila is the product of a cultural blend: in this case, of native Mexican agave and European-imported stills. The Hernández family is proud to have created this tequila in a symbolic return to Mexico's Spanish roots.

La Cofradía, S.A. de C.V.
Calle La Cofradía s/n,
46400 Tequila, Jalisco.
T. (33) 367 32443 / F. (33) 367 32492
cofradia@mpsnet.com.mx

Sauza Conmemorativo

For 125 years the Sauza family has proudly produced this genuine, quality tequila that constitutes a true Mexican tradition, even bringing to mind a certain song: "My soul is drunk on tequila eternally, to see if that will cure its cruel melancholy." Sauza Conmemorativo is an añejo tequila.

Tequila Sauza, S.A. de C.V.
Av. Vallarta 3273, Colonia Vallarta Poniente,
44110 Guadalajara, Jalisco.
T. (33) 367 90600 / F. (33) 367 90691

Siete leguas

Siete Leguas was by far Pancho Villa's favorite steed. Whenever it heard the train whistle, it would rear up and neigh. This tequila's potency and feistiness render homage to the horse belonging to Villa, the Centaur of the North, a figure much admired by Ignacio González, who created this brand in 1950. It is elaborated in Atotonilco el Alto using a traditional *tahona* mill.

Tequila Siete Leguas, S.A. de C.V.
Mariposa 1139, Colonia Jardines de la Victoria,
44530 Guadalajara, Jalisco.
T. (33) 367 12064

Tequila 1910

The Mexican Revolution started in 1910, and Tequila 1910 had its origin during the same period. This 100% agave tequila was created in homage to that episode in Mexican history. That year, it was produced with home stills in the region of Santo Tomás, Jalisco, to enliven family gatherings held by Zenaido and Benigno Galván. The blown-glass bottle is a replica of the ones used during the Revolution.

La Cofradía, S.A. de C.V.
Av. de los Novelistas 5063, Jardines Vallarta,
45027 Zapopan, Jalisco.
T. (33) 361 42517
lacofradia@infosel.net.mx

Tequila 30-30

In the opinion of some experts, the best *Agave tequilana Weber*, blue variety, grows in Los Altos of Jalisco, where Capilla de Guadalupe is located. Certain features of this area such as the altitude and the rich, moist soil combine to produce an excellent 100% agave tequila, bottled on-site.

Agroindustria Guadalajara, S.A. de C.V.
San Rafael 344, Colonia Chapadita,
45030 Guadalajara, Jalisco.
T. (33) 364 76400 / F. (33) 312 29788
http://www.3030tequila.com

Tres Alegres Compadres

This reposado tequila was created in 1992 in Tequila, Jalisco, under the careful supervision of the Hernández family. Its name refers to three men who are *compadres* in real life, one of whom is the owner of the La Cofradía distillery.

La Cofradía, S.A. de C.V.
Calle La Cofradía s/n,
46400 Tequila, Jalisco.
T. (33) 367 32443 / F. (33) 367 32492
cofradia@mpsnet.com.mx

Tres Generaciones

This fine tequila pertains to the great Sauza family reserve. The Sauza family has three generations of experience in the production of tequila, hence the name of this brand: Tres Generaciones. In 1873, the company's founder Cenobio Sauza acquired the La Antigua Cruz distillery, which was rebaptized La Perseverancia fifteen years later, as depicted in a splendid mural by painter Gabriel Flores.

Tequila Sauza, S.A. de C.V.
Av. Vallarta 3273, Colonia Vallarta Poniente,
44110 Guadalajara, Jalisco.
T. (33) 367 90600 / F. (3) 367 90691

Don Julio

Don Julio González shares a legend with us when we partake of this pure liquor extracted from the agaves of Atotonilco el Alto. Initially produced for the exclusive consumption of friends and family, it is available to the public in three presentations: blanco, reposado and añejo, and is best served neat. This company, founded in 1942, also produces Tres Magueyes Reposado and Tres Magueyes Blanco.

Tequila Don Julio
Calz. Lázaro Cárdenas 3289, Tercer piso.
Col. Chapalita.
45000 Guadalajara, Jalisco.
T. (33) 3647 8775, (33) 3121 9252

Elixires de Agave

Don Maximiliano Añejo

This *elixir de agave*, bottled for the first time in 1990, is aged for at least two years. After selecting the finest agaves in the Los Altos region of Jalisco, Alberto Becherano takes personal responsibility for maintaining Don Maximiliano Añejo's excellent quality. The bottle's classic design is sober and elegant, emphasizing the product's regal image.

Tequilas de la Doña, S.A. de C.V.
Tlapexco 25, Colonia Palo Alto,
05110 Mexico City
T. (55) 525 95432 / F. (55) 525 95449
elixirdeagave@hotmail.com

El Capricho Añejo

The blue agave could be considered a *capricho* or whim of nature, as it can only be found in a very small part of the world. This was the origin of the name of this *elixir de agave*, launched in 1997. An elixir de agave differs from a tequila in that it has only thirty-six percent alcohol by volume, giving it a balanced flavor that is appealing to all.

El Capricho Maduro

This *elixir de agave* was created by Alberto Becherano, who personally supervises every stage of the production process. El Capricho Maduro was released in 1998, offering the public an alternative characterized by the four- to five-month aging period needed for an elixir to reach full maturity.

Don Maximiliano Reposado

The name of this product denotes rank, and recalls majestic nineteenth-century Mexico. Unlike tequila, a reposado *elixir de agave* ages for another six months after maturing, a process that requires four to six months. The bottle's classic design and elegant label are true to the brand's sophisticated image.

El Capricho Reposado

To achieve the velvety flavor of this *elixir de agave*, the tequila is aged for a further six months after the four- to six-month period required for it to reach maturity. Its balance and generous bouquet are clear proof of the infinite merits of the agave.

Reserva del Emperador

The name of this elixir sets a standard of quality as it announces an intention to create a drink fit for an emperor. Master-craftsman Alonso González was commissioned to design and fabricate by hand 220 numbered and signed decanters—a fitting container for this exclusive and limited reserve.

Liqueur and Sangrita

Sangrita Viuda de Sánchez

The legend of José Sánchez goes back to the early 1920s. He enjoyed entertaining friends with a good tequila, accompanied by an exquisite chaser prepared by his wife, Guadalupe Nuño. She later took over the business and popularized this beverage—the original sangrita—around Mexico under her own name: Viuda de Sánchez, or Sánchez's widow. Made from fresh oranges or orange juice, salt and *chiles de árbol*, this is tequila's inseparable companion.

Casa Cuervo, S.A. de C.V.
Av. Churubusco 213, Colonia Granjas,
08400 Mexico City
T. / F. (55) 580 32400

La Pinta

La Pinta is a fine pomegranate and tequila liqueur manufactured from natural fruit juices, quality tequila, and natural sweeteners. Once prepared, it is stored for six months in glass carafes, in a strictly controlled environment. La Pinta was named after one of the first ships to reach America from the Mediterranean port of Palos. It symbolizes the junction of the Mexican and Spanish cultures, as reflected in the bottle's design.

Casa Tradición, S.A. de C.V.
Rosario 611-208, Colonia Jardines de los Arcos,
44520 Guadalajara, Jalisco.
T. / F. (33) 364 73250
lapinta@mexicobiz.com

V

Reference

Directory of Distilleries

Agave Tequilana Productores y Comercializadores, S.A. de C.V.
Rincón de las Acacias 122 F,
Rinconada del Sol,
45050 Zapopan, Jalisco.
T. +52 (33) 3122 7206
F. +52 (33) 3647 7144
agavetequilana@infosel.mx.net

Agaveros Unidos de Amatitán, S.A. de C.V.
Rancho Miravalle s/n,
45380 Amatitán, Jalisco.
T./F. +52 (374) 745 0781

Agroindustria Guadalajara, S.A.
Extramuros 504,
Capilla de Guadalupe, Jalisco.
T. +52 (378) 712 1515, 712 1210
F. +52 (378) 712 1331
htlenrique@mexis.com

Casa Barrueco, S.A. de C.V.
Pichón 1500 B,
44810 Guadalajara, Jalisco.
T. +52 (33) 3812 0594
F. +52 (33) 3811 0099

Casa Cuervo, S.A. de C.V.
Periférico Sur 8500,
Tramo Morelia Chapala,
45601 Tlaquepaque, Jalisco.
T. +52 (33) 3134 3300
F. +52 (33) 3634 4298
eaguila@cuervo.com.mx

Catador Alteño, S.A. de C.V.
Rancho Los Ladrillos,
Carr. Jesús María km 1.5,
47950 Jesús María, Jalisco.
T. +52 (348) 704 0277
F. +52 (348) 704 0227
catadoralteno@megared.net.mx

Cía. Destiladora de Acatlán, S.A. de C.V.
Independencia 157,
Col. La Calma 45700,
Acatlán de Juárez, Jalisco.
T. +52 (387) 772 0177

Cía. Tequilera de Arandas, S.A. de C.V.
Portal Allende 1 int. 2,
Centro, entre Morelos y Madero,
47180 Arandas, Jalisco.
T. +52 (348) 784 5440
F. +52 (348) 783 0763

Corporación Ansan, S.A. de C.V.
Juan Ruiz de Alarcón 127,
44140 Guadalajara, Jalisco.
T./F. +52 (33) 3630 2022

Destiladora Azteca de Jalisco, S.A. de C.V.
Silverio Núñez 108,
46400 Tequila, Jalisco.
T. +52 (374) 74 202 46
F. +52 (374) 74 207 19

Destiladora González González, S.A. de C.V.
Puerto Altata 1131,
44330 Guadalajara, Jalisco.
T. +52 (33) 3637 8484
F. +52 (33) 3651 5397

Destiladora La Barranca, S.A. de C.V.
Independencia 73,
47600 Tepatitlán, Jalisco.
T./F. +52 (378) 782 1467
jarroviejo@tepa.com.mx

Destiladora Los Magos, S.A. de C.V.
Av. de las Margaritas 177,
Jardines de la Calera,
45645 Tlajomulco de Zúñiga, Jalisco.
T./F. +52 (33) 3161 5854
losmagos@mixmail.com

Destiladora San Nicolás, S.A. de C.V.
Camino Real Atotonilco 1061,
47180 Arandas, Jalisco.
T./F. +52 (348) 781 0012

Destilería Santa Cruz
Santa Cruz,
Plazuela del Himno Nacional, 5-A,
46400 Tequila, Jalisco.
T. +52 (374) 742 2123, 742 2126
F. +52 (374) 742 2124

Destilerías Unidas, S.A. de C.V.
Puerto Altata 1131 int. 2,
44330 Guadalajara, Jalisco.
T. +52 (33) 3637 8484
F. +52 (33) 3651 5397
destiladoragg@megared.net.mx

Empresa Ejidal Tequilera Amatitán
Camino a la Barranca
del Tecuane s/n,
45380 Amatitán, Jalisco.
T. +52 (374) 745 0043
F. +52 (374) 745 0549

**Fábrica de Aguardientes de Agave
La Mexicana, S.A. de C.V.**
Rancho Llano Grande,
Carr. Arandas-León km 2.5,
47180 Arandas, Jalisco.
T. +52 (348) 784 6051
F. +52 (348) 784 6001
temexico@cysc.sienega.com.mx

**Feliciano Vivanco y Asociados,
S.A. de C.V.**
Carr. Arandas-Tepatitlán km 2,
47180 Arandas, Jalisco.
T./F. +52 (348) 783 0780

**Grupo Industrial Tequilero
de Los Altos de Jalisco, S.A. de C.V.**
Carr. Arandas-Tepatitlán km 17.5,
47180 Arandas, Jalisco.
T./F. +52 (348) 716 0317 , 716 0318

**Grupo Internacional de Exportación,
S.A. de C.V.**
Mariano Otero 3433-304, 45060
Guadalajara, Jalisco.
T. +52 (33) 3643 7232
F. +52 (33) 3647 9597

Grupo Tequilero México, S.A. de C.V.
Carr. Jesús María-Ayotlán km 1.5,
Jesús María, Jalisco.
T. +52 (348) 704 0028
F. +52 (348) 704 0007

**Industrializadora de Agave San
Isidro, S.A. de C.V.**
Camino Tepatitlán-San José de
Gracia km 2,
Tepatitlán de Morelos, Jalisco.
T./F. +52 (378) 782 20 06

JDC, S.A. de C.V.
Av. del Tequila 1,
47180 Arandas, Jalisco.
T. +52 (348) 784 5973
F. +52 (348) 784 5966
maria_elena_ascencio@seagra.com

Jorge Michel Padilla
Carr. Autlán-Cd. Guzmán, Crucero
San Juan de Amula, 48700, Municipio
de Limón, Jalisco.
T. +52 (33) 3373 0032
F. +52 (33) 3373 0250

**Jorge Salles Cuervo y Suc.,
S.A. de C.V.**
Leandro Valle 991,
44100 Guadalajara, Jalisco.
T. +52 (33) 3614 9400
F. +52 (33) 3613 0169

La Arandina, S.A. de C.V.
Periférico Norte, Lateral Sur 762,
45150 Zapopan, Jalisco.
T. +52 (33) 3636 2430
F. +52 (33) 3656 2176

La Cofradía, S.A. de C.V.
Av. de los Novelistas 5063,
Jardines Vallarta,
45027 Zapopan, Jalisco.
T. +52 (33) 3614 2517
lacofradia@infosel.net.mx

La Madrileña, S.A. de C.V.
Arroz 89, Col. Santa Isabel Industrial,
09820, México D.F.
T. +52 (55) 5582 2222

Milemiglia, S.A. de C.V.
Bosques de Ciruelos 162,
Bosques de Chapultepec,
11700 México, D.F.
T. +52 (55) 5203 7836
F. +52 (55) 5545 2122

Pernod Ricard México, S.A. de C.V.
Homero 440 Int. 401,
Col. Polanco,
11560 México, D.F.
T. +52 (55) 5255 4623
F. +52 (55) 5255 4526

Procesadora de Agave Pénjamo
Camelinas 2,
36900 Pénjamo, Guanajuato.
T. +52 (469) 692 2450
F. +52 (569) 692 2895

**Productos Finos de Agave,
S.A. de C.V.**
Carr. Jesús María-Ayotlán km 1.5,
47950 Jesús María, Jalisco.
T. +52 (370) 407 0007
F. +52 (370) 400 28

Ruth Ledesma Macías
Dr. Mateo el Regil 49,
Col. El Briseño,
45230 Zapopan, Jalisco.
T./F. +52 (33) 3684 5142

**Tequila Artesanal
de Los Altos de Jalisco, S.A. de C.V.**
Rancho Agua Fría s/n,
47755 Atotonilco el Alto, Jalisco.
T./F. +52 (393) 931 7304

**Tequila Caballito Cerrero,
S.A. de C.V.**
Simón Bolívar 186,
44140 Guadalajara, Jalisco.
T. +52 (33) 3615 1338
F. +52 (33) 3616 0023

Tequila Cascahuín, S.A. de C.V.
Hospital 423,
44280 Guadalajara, Jalisco.
T./F. +52 (33) 3614 9958

Tequila Cazadores, S.A. de C.V.
Carr. Arandas-Tepa km 1, 47180
Arandas, Jalisco.
T. +52 (348) 784 5570
F. +52 (348) 451 89

Tequila Centinela, S.A. de C.V.
Carr. Arandas-Tepa km 2.5,
47180 Arandas, Jalisco.
T. +52 (378) 304 68
F. +52 (378) 309 33

Tequila Cuervo, S.A. de C.V.
Periférico Sur 8500,
tramo Morelia-Chapala,
45601 Tlaquepaque, Jalisco.
T. +52 (33) 3134 3300
F. +52 (33) 3644 4298

Tequila Don Julio, S.A. de C.V.
Calz. Lázaro Cárdenas 3289, 3° piso
45000 Guadalajara, Jalisco.
T. +52 (33) 3647 8775
T. +52 (33) 3121 9252

Tequila El Viejito, S.A. de C.V.
Eucalipto 2234,
44900 Guadalajara, Jalisco.
T. +52 (33) 3812 9092
F. +52 (33) 3812 9590

Tequila La Herradura, S.A. de C.V.
Av. 16 de Septiembre 635, Centro,
44180 Guadalajara, Jalisco.
T. +52 (33) 3942 3900

**Tequila Orendain de Jalisco,
S.A. de C.V.**
Av. Vallarta 6230,
45010 Zapopan, Jalisco.
T. +52 (33) 3627 1827
F. +52 (33) 3777 1810

Tequila La Parreñita, S.A. de C.V.
Av. Alcalde 859,
42280 Guadalajara, Jalisco.
T./F. +52 (33) 3613 6076

Tequila Quiote, S.A. de C.V.
Extramuros 502,
San Francisco de Asís,
47750 Atotonilco el Alto, Jalisco.
T./F. +52 (391) 931 7080

Tequila R.G., S.A. de C.V.
Madero 37,
46400 Tequila, Jalisco.
T./F. +52 (33) 3628 6541

**Tequila San Matías de Jalisco,
S.A. de C.V.**
Calderón de la Barca 177,
44100 Guadalajara, Jalisco.
T./F. +52 (33) 3615 0421
ventas@sanmatias.com.mx

Tequila Santa Fe, S.A. de C.V.
Calz. Gobernador Curiel 1708,
44910 Guadalajara, Jalisco.
T. +52 (33) 3811 7588
F. +52 (33) 3811 7903
santafe@ram.com.mx

Tequila Sauza, S.A. de C.V.
Av. Vallarta 6503,
Centro Comercial Concentro 49
zona E,
Col. Ciudad Granjas,
45010 Zapopan, Jalisco.
T. +52 (33) 3679 0600
F. +52 (33) 3679 0691

Tequila Sierra Brava, S.A. de C.V.
Aldama 200,
El Salvador,
46400 Tequila, Jalisco.
T. +52 (33) 3620 4583
sierrabrava@prodigy.net.mx

Tequila Siete Leguas, S.A. de C.V.
Mariposas 1139,
44530 Guadalajara, Jalisco.
T./F. +52 (33) 3671 2064
tequila7leguas@hotmail.com

Tequila Supremo, S.A. de C.V.
Periférico Norte, Lateral Sur 762,
45150 Zapopan, Jalisco.
T. +52 (33) 3636 2557
F. +52 (33) 3656 2176

Tequila Tapatío, S.A. de C.V.
Álvaro Obregón 35,
470180 Arandas, Jalisco.
T. +52 (348) 783 0425
F. +52 (348) 783 1666

Tequila Tres Mujeres, S.A. de C.V.
Carr. interior Guadalajara-Nogales
km 39, 45380 Amatitán, Jalisco.
T./F. +52 (374) 748 0140
tequilatresmujeres@hotmail.com

Tequilas del Señor, S.A. de C.V.
Río Tuito 1193,
44870 Guadalajara, Jalisco
T. +52 (33) 3837 0440
F. +52 (33) 3837 0430

Tequila de La Doña, S.A. de C.V.
Tlapesco 25,
Col. Palo Alto,
05110 Cuajimalpa, México D.F.
T. +52 (55) 5259 5432
elixirdeagave@hotmail.com

Tequileña, S.A. de C.V.
Venezuela 425,
Col. Americana,
44600 Guadalajara, Jalisco.
T./F. +52 (33) 3825 9329
legal@tequilena.com.mx

Tequila Corralejo, S.A. de C.V.
Carr. San Martín Tepajaco km 2.5,
col. San Martín Tepatlixpán,
54763 Cuautitlán Izcalli, Estado de
México.
T. +52 (55) 5877 0203
F. +52 (55) 5877 0334

Tequila La Gonzaleña, S.A. de C.V.
Darwin 68,
Col. Anzures,
5590 Mexico D.F.
T. +52 (55) 5531 5959
F. +52 (55) 5531 8826

Tequilera de El Salto, S.A. de C.V.
Calle A 12-B Parque Industrial,
45681 El Salto, Jalisco.
T. +52 (33) 3688 1457

Tequilera Don Roberto, S.A. de C.V.
Carr. Interior 100 Oriente,
46400 Tequila, Jalisco.
T./F. +52 (374) 742 2321

**Tequilera Newton e Hijos,
S.A. de C.V.**
Ruperto Salas 168,
Col. Benito Juárez,
45190 Zapopan, Jalisco.
T./F. +52 (33) 3660 2945

Other Useful Addresses

**Unión de Productores de Agave
(Union of Agave Producers)**
Melchor Ocampo 18,
Centro,
46400 Tequila, Jalisco.
T./F. +52 (374) 7421 600

**Consejo Regulador del Tequila
(Tequila Regulatory Council)**
Calle Herodes 2619,
Jardines del Bosque,
44520 Guadalajara, Jalisco.
T. +52 (33) 3647 5905
F. +52 (33) 3647 6148
www.crt.org.mx

**Cámara Nacional de la Industria
Tequilera (National Chamber
of the Tequila Industry)**
Lázaro Cárdenas 3289, piso 5,
45000 Guadalajara, Jalisco.
T. +52 (33) 3121 5021
F. +52 (33) 3647 2031
www.camaratequilera.com.mx

Glossary

Agave sazón
Mature agave. The maturing period lasts from seven to twelve years.

Agave deserti
Ranchers in Baja California prepare their regional beverage using this agave whose leaves grow only to thirty centimeters in length.

Agave potatorum
Bacanora, the mezcal made in Sonora, comes from this plant.

Alambique
"Still." Pressurized apparatus for distilling tequila.

Alquitara
Slow distillation.

Barbeo
To cut or trim the tips of the fleshy leaves of the agave. This is a kind of pruning that is thought to increase the size of the head or root of the maguey.

Barbeo de escobeta
"Brush cut." A form of pruning that induces an early maturation of the plant.

Batidor
"Beater." A worker who gets into the vats naked and beats the must with his hands and feet to remove the fibers from the crushed agave leaves.

Botija
A potbellied clay bottle with a short, narrow neck. It was made from goat leather. Used as a measure for retail sale, seven botijas equal a barrel.

Chicotuda
An agave plant with a somewhat unhealthy appearance, as if it were old and tired.

Chinguirito
Mexican liquors made from sugar cane. Also, mezcal plants that in the eighteenth and nineteenth centuries were widely considered to be of low quality.

Coa de jima
A tool used in harvesting, like a long, narrow, sharp-edged spade.

Cogollo
"Sprout, top." An appendage growing from the upper part of the *piña*, that sprouts from the *mezontle*. This is where the agave plant originates.

Condensador
"Condenser." A kind of metal snake where the vapors produced by cooling during distillation are condensed.

Damajuana
"Demijohn." A commercial unit of measure for retail sale (8 1/2 gallons). It consisted of a potbellied glass container covered in wicker and with handles.

Desquiote
When the agave flower is cut to keep the plant from dying.

Destilación
"Distillation." The process by which the alcohol is extracted from the fermented juice.

Fermentación
"Fermentation." The process by which the reductive sugars in the juice are transformed into ethyl alcohol.

Hervidor
"Boiler." In certain kinds of water-heaters, the tube where the water boils.

Hijuelo
Small plant that sprouts at the base of the agave and is pulled when it is a year old.

Huachicol
A drink spiked with alcohol, especially cane alcohol.

Ixtle
A textile fiber extracted from the blue agave to make rope. Also known as *pita*.

238

Jima
The operation by which the agave leaves are stripped from the plant and the piña is uprooted from the ground.

Limpia
"Cleaning." Weeding and loosening the soil around the agave plant using the *coa*, clearing a space about fifty inches wide around each plant.

Manolarga
A large agave with leaves that are greener and stand up straighter than other species.

Marrana
Dried mezcal fiber.

Melgas
The space between an agave field's furrows, used to sow corn or beans when the plants are still small.

Mezontle, Mesonte
The center of a mezcal piña. It has a grainy texture.

Mezcal
A plant used to make tequila or mezcal. Also, a regional beverage obtained from the agave plant, similar to tequila.

Mosto
"Must." Juice of the agave or any fruit that is fermented to produce alcohol.

Nitzicuile
A worm that destroys the agave root.

Paloma
A disease that rots the leaves of the mezcal plant.

Penca
The fleshy leaf of the agave plant.

Perla or Concha
"Pearl" or "shell." The bubble that remains on the tequila's surface after pouring or shaking it.

Pipones
Wooden recipients that generally hold eighty barrels or about 1400 gallons, though there are other sizes.

Potrero
"Pasture." In Tequila, an agave plantation, also known as *tren* (train), *rancho* (ranch) or *huerto* (orchard).

Quiote
Stalk that sprouts from the heart of the maguey; the maguey flower. Boiled or roasted whole, it is very nutritious and has a unique sweet flavor.

Taberna
Tequila distillery. Also, a store where tequila is sold in bulk.

Tahona
Circular space lined with masonry around which a stone wheel is pulled by a team of mules or oxen.

Tatemar
To cook the agave piña to concentrate all the sugars that will later be fermented and distilled.

Tequio
"Work." The word tequila may have derived from this term.

Tequila cortado
"Cut tequila." A tequila that, when shaken in the bottle, does not produce the *perla* or *concha* so coveted by connoisseurs.

Tequila de hornitos
Elaborated from *tuba* in a copper vessel. The vessel is covered with a piece of wood, filling in any cracks with clay. The condenser is a wooden coil.

Tonel
A wooden recipient for transporting liquids. An antiquated measurement equivalent to about 380 pounds.

Tuba
Recently distilled tequila with a sweetish flavor. Also, a liquor obtained from palm.

Translated by Michelle Suderman.

Tequila

Editors: Alberto Ruy-Sánchez, Margarita de Orellana
Guest Editor: Eliot Weinberger
Editorial Coordinators: Michelle Suderman, Gabriela Olmos
Design: Leonardo Vázquez
Translators: Susan Briante, John T. O'Brien, Mark Schafer, Lorna Scott Fox,
Sara Silver, Michelle Suderman, Christopher Winks
Copy Editing: Robert Poarch
Design Assistants: Daniel Moreno, Aidee Santiago, Mariana Zúñiga
Prepress: Alejandro Pérez Mainou

Photography:

Galería Agustín Cristóbal:
pp. 111–112, 116–117.
Ricardo Garibay: p. 171.
Instituto Mexicano de Cinematografía:
pp. 140–141, 144–145, 146, 148–149, 155, 181, 184–185.
M. Claudio Jiménez Vizcarra:
pp. 108–109, 118, 121.
Patricia Tamés:
pp. 13, 122–123.
Jorge Vértiz:
pp. 6 to 10, 14 to 17, 41, 46–47, 49, 51, 52, 55, 58–59, 70–71, 83,
87, 90–91, 94, 100 to 105, 115, 125, 126, 128, 131 to 133, 135, 138–139,
147, 151, 152, 157, 159, 160, 162–163, 165, 166, 169, 172, 177, 183, 186,
187, 200 to 204, 228, 229, 232, 234, 235.

Illustrations:

Ruth Rodríguez, Luis Vargas, Joel Rendón
Recipes section: Elena Climent

Acknowledgements:

Archivo General de la Nación
Consejo Regulador del Tequila
Filmoteca UNAM
Galería Agustín Cristóbal
Instituto Mexicano de Cinematografía
José Cuervo y Compañía
Juan Beckmann Vidal
Juan Domingo Beckmann
Andrea Huerta
Claudio Jiménez Vizcarra
Laura Martínez
Ricardo Pérez Escamilla
Samantha Ogazón